Flying the
Airbus

A380

Flying the Airbus
A380

Captain Gib Vogel

Airlife

First published in 2009 by
The Crowood Press Ltd
Ramsbury, Marlborough
Wiltshire SN8 2HR

www.crowood.com

This impression 2011

British Library Cataloguing-in-Publication Data
A catalogue record for this book is available from the British Library.

ISBN 978 1 84797 124 1

Acknowledgements
Completing his book would not have been possible without the help of my friends
and colleagues, who unselfishly provided photographs and contributed information
for the text. I would especially like to thank Stanley Stewart, author of *Flying the Big
Jets* (Crowood), whose literary guidance helped me in the organization and preparation of the manuscript. Stan's help and contributions were invaluable; without him,
the book would not have seen the light of day.

Cover photos: Hushouyan

Edited and designed by Ian Penberthy

Printed and bound in China by Leo Paper Products

CONTENTS

FOREWORD

As an airline pilot and aviation author of many years, I have long been aware of the interest in aviation among the general public. Myriad books have been written on the subject, from enthusiast booklets to technical manuals, and from specialized military fighter publications to magazines on airliners, but few catch the interest of layman and professional alike. This book does.

Flying the A380 has been written by a senior A380 captain, whose first-hand knowledge of what it is actually like to fly the giant aircraft brings the subject alive. The reader can get a sense of being part of the crew and is introduced to the sophistication of the cockpit displays in a way that can be appreciated by all, whether interested layperson, enthusiast or aviation professional.

The A380 has a massive maximum take-off weight of 570,000kg (1,256,000lb) and can carry up to 850 economy-class passengers in a double-decker layout; from the planning stage, its enormous size fired the imagination of the public. Reports of on-board lounge bars and discos, and even swimming pools and gyms, stretched reality a little too far and ignored commercial pressures, never mind the weight of water and exercise equipment! In the main, airlines have adopted a maximum of about 470 passengers in a three-class layout that allows comfortable travel for all. First-class passengers are also able to enjoy small lounges, separate cabins and beds, and, in one configuration, fitted showers.

At every air show where an A380 is on display, large numbers of people gather to gaze in amazement at its vast bulk; whenever it took to the air during its development, huge crowds flocked to watch. Interest in the A380's first flight drew 50,000 spectators, and seats on the inaugural commercial flight with Singapore Airlines, from Singapore to Sydney in October 2007, were auctioned on eBay. Such was the appeal of the historic occasion that a total of US$1.3 million was raised and donated by the airline to charities.

What is the giant A380 like to fly, however? What is the detail of the flight-deck presentation; what are the functions of the sophisticated cockpit displays; and how is the aircraft operated? Until now, such information has been the preserve of those few privileged professional pilots who have been given the chance to fly the huge machine. In *Flying the A380*, however, all have the opportunity to see the cockpit at close range and to experience a trip on the flight deck of this magnificent aeroplane.

Stanley Stewart
Author, Flying the Big Jets

INTRODUCTION

Before I started my conversion training for the Airbus A380 in early 2008, I began scouring the bookshops and Internet for a book that would tell me about the aircraft. As I had flown only American made Boeings previously, I expected that it would be a challenge to adapt to the concepts and intricacies of flying the European made A380, and I wanted an oversight of the aircraft's operations and systems. I was unsuccessful, however, as all I found were a few books on the development of the aircraft. Presumably, this was due to the fact that it had been introduced into service only recently, in late 2007.

After my successful conversion to the aircraft, I decided to put right this lack of information by writing my own book on its operations and systems, to introduce both pilots and aviation enthusiasts alike to the A380. I have based the book on a typical flight from London to Dubai, and have explained the operations and different systems of the aircraft along the way. The story also covers the latest in airliner operations in terms of air traffic and cockpit management.

It is my hope that this book will provide a good overview of the operations and concepts of the newest and largest passenger aircraft in the world, the Airbus A380.

Captain Gib Vogel,
February 2009

CHAPTER 1
PRE-FLIGHT

The flight crew pauses by the steps of the Airbus A380 before boarding and, as they glance up at the massive fuselage, they briefly contemplate the enormous size of the aircraft. With a wingspan of 79.8m (261.8ft), a height of 24.1m (79.1ft) and a length of 73.0m (239.5ft), it looks big and stubby on the apron. The Airbus A380 is 15m (49ft) wider and 2m (6.5ft) longer than the Boeing 747, and is the biggest commercial airliner in the world. It has an incredible maximum take-off weight of 570 tonnes (561imp/628US tons), compared to the 397 tonnes (391imp/438US tons) of the passenger-carrying 747-400, a maximum range of 8,200nm (15,200km) and a maximum altitude of 43,000ft.

FLIGHT PLANNING

Two or three hours before arriving at the aircraft, in a comfortable hotel room, the captain of this flight, Skybird 380 from London Heathrow to Dubai, would have logged on to the Internet to access the flight plan for perusal. Around four hours before scheduled departure, the flight planning department at the airline's home base in Dubai would have chosen the most suitable routing and filed an Air Traffic Control (ATC) flight plan for the trip. This plan would also have been filed with the first en-route air traffic control centre, the Central Flow Management Unit (CFMU) at Eurocontrol, which, in turn, would have forwarded it by telex to the other air traffic centres along the route, in Romania, Turkey and Iran.

Route-search computer programs, such as Lufthansa's 'LIDO', British Airways' 'STAR' and Continental Airlines' 'Phoenix', display the most cost-effective routes for nominated departure and arrival airports. Flight routing costs, such as fuel, aircraft time and air traffic control charges, are included for consideration, but excluded are variable costs, such as catering and amenities, staffing and landing fees. Fuel cost, however, is the overriding factor, and on long-haul flights it accounts for 90 per cent of total basic flight routing costs (75 per cent on short-haul flights). Essentially, air traffic control charges are time based – the longer the over-flight, the more the airline pays – and vary across Europe. For example, on the flight described in this book, the charge for over-flying the Slovak Republic was US$400, while crossing Romania cost US$1,700.

Winds aloft along the route are also an important factor in the calculations,

An Airbus A380 on the apron. The enormous passenger aircraft towers over everything in its vicinity.

as they affect flight time and, consequently, fuel burn. With the high cost of fuel, it is not surprising, therefore, that the shortest flight-time route is usually the best option. Having selected the most cost-effective routing, the dispatcher checks the en-route weather for significant forecasts and the relevant Notices to Airmen (NOTAMS) to verify the suitability of the routing. NOTAMS are published by national aviation authorities and list abnormal circumstances that may affect flight through their respective airspaces, alerting pilots to such situations as inoperative radio beacons, closed airport facilities and specific airspace closures for military exercises and similar activities.

Also collated by the dispatcher is information prepared by the airline's traffic specialists on the expected load, including passenger and cargo distribution, and the aircraft serviceability status, which is provided by engineering central control. These items, plus the weather reports, NOTAMS and copies of the ATC flight plan, flight log and fuel log, form a flight planning briefing package that is uploaded to the Internet for pilot access. A copy of the package is also sent to the airline's departure dispatch office, in this case in London.

In the airline's London office, the local dispatcher confirms the availability of the selected route with Eurocontrol and checks the allocated take-off time, known as the 'slot time'. To co-ordinate aircraft joining the busy airway system aloft, all flights departing European airports are allocated a slot time with which the pilots are required to comply. If the selected routing is unavailable, or if the allocated slot time creates an excessive departure delay, another suitable route would be requested from the Dubai dispatch office and a fresh flight plan filed. These ATC slot times are not to be confused with airport slot times, which are negotiated and traded by airlines months earlier to schedule their departures from this busy airport.

Weather is also checked by the captain, using terminal aerodrome forecasts (TAFs), which give forecasts for the coming twenty-four hours for all the required en-route, destination and alternate (diversion) airports. For this flight, the captain observes that no adverse weather is reported for the night-time arrival at Dubai. The city's weather is usually clear, but occasionally morning fog or sandstorms occur, and subsequently the low visibility can be a cause for concern. Dubai airport charts, produced by Jeppesen, form part of the Electronic Flight Bag (EFB) on the flight deck and give the minimum visibility required for the arrival.

The captain scans the NOTAMS for anything that could have an adverse effect on the flight. Information is presented for the entire route and can be extensive, but pilots become skilful at picking out notices of concern as they glance through the many pages, saving, perhaps, an hour of reading. Any notices concerning the departure, destination and alternate airports are scrutinized a little more carefully, however, while the remainder of the NOTAMS can be read in more detail during the cruise.

Fuel Requirement

When deciding the final fuel figure, factors such as possible delays resulting from busy traffic at arrival time, air traffic control procedures, or poor destination or en-route weather need to be considered and may require extra fuel to be carried. For example, delays can be expected when arriving at Heathrow during the peak evening period, thus justifying the carriage of additional fuel. Pilots are aware of the high cost of fuel, however, and endeavour not to uplift more than necessary. Taking additional fuel can be not only costly, but also wasteful, as on long flights it is expected that half the extra fuel will be burned just carrying that extra fuel. That is to say, for every extra 1,000kg of fuel loaded, 500kg will be burned off in carrying the extra weight on a long flight, leaving only 500kg for use at the destination.

To prevent airlines from taking too little fuel, however, aviation law dictates that a minimum amount must be carried for each flight. The minimum fuel load comprises:

- *Burn-Off* – Fuel used for the flight.
- *Contingency Fuel* – Additional fuel to safeguard against unexpected circumstances, equal to 5 per cent of the burn-off (this may be reduced to 3 per cent if approved by the local authorities) plus sufficient fuel to reach a mandatory alternate airport.
- *Reserve Fuel* – For holding.
- *Taxi Fuel*.

The Zero Fuel Weight (ZFW) – the weight of the aircraft, crew, passengers, baggage and cargo, but without fuel – of the A380 for this particular flight is

355.0 tonnes (349.4imp/391.3US tons); the burn-off for the six-hour flight is 74.0 tonnes (72.8imp/81.6US tons); the fuel load for contingency, alternate and reserve is 14.9 tonnes (14.7imp/16.4US tons); and the taxi fuel is 1.5 tonnes (1.5imp/1.7US tons), giving a total minimum flight-plan fuel requirement for refuelling the aircraft of 90.4 tonnes (89.0imp/99.6US tons) and a total taxi weight of 445.4 tonnes (438.4imp/491.0US tons). The taxi weight minus the taxi fuel of 1.5 tonnes gives a take-off weight of 443.9 tonnes (436.9imp/489.3US tons), and the take-off weight minus the burn-off gives an expected landing weight of 369.9 tonnes (364.1imp/407.7US tons). The captain considers that the satisfactory weather forecast and other factors do not justify loading extra fuel, and he accepts the minimum flight-plan fuel required of 90.4 tonnes.

DATA TRANSFER

Having made the decision, the captain calls the London dispatch office to approve the planned routing and the requirement for flight-plan fuel. The approved flight plan and other briefing documents are datalinked to the aircraft's EFB as an 'e-folder' (electronic folder) at least one hour before flight departure, allowing the crew to bypass the dispatch office on arrival at the airport and proceed directly to the aircraft. Before boarding, however, the pilots will need to collect a hard copy of the flight briefing package, and the captain will be required to initial a flight-plan summary that will be returned to the dispatch office. The hard copy of the briefing package is carried in case of EFB failure, and good airmanship dictates that the pilots keep a running log of progress, filling in the flight details on the paper flight log as the aircraft progresses along the route. Thus if the EFB does fail, the pilots can fall back on the updated manual flight log. On most flights, however, this practice becomes somewhat academic, as all the flight details are recorded electronically and the hard copy is simply discarded at the end of the trip.

Datalink messaging is used extensively for the transfer of data between the aircraft and ground units, and is sent and received via the on-board Aircraft Communications Addressing and Reporting System (ACARS). ACARS transmissions are sent via radio or by satellite communication (Satcom), allowing the easy transfer of data between the aircraft and airline operations, weather service providers and ATC centres.

CREW ARRIVAL

As the two cockpit crew travel on the bus to the airport, they take the opportunity to discuss the briefing they have both checked earlier on the Internet. On arrival, the bus takes them to an airside perimeter gate for the routine security screening process before driving them directly to the aircraft. By the time they arrive, about forty-five minutes remain before the scheduled departure of the Skybird 380 service from London to Dubai.

CHAPTER 2
BIRTH OF
THE A380

The super jumbo was conceived in the mid-eighties, when the two big aircraft manufacturers, Airbus and Boeing, contemplated the need for a very large passenger aircraft. While European builder Airbus pursued the idea of an aircraft that could carry as many as 800 people, across the Atlantic, Boeing decided on another strategy. It set out to design smaller, but longer-range planes that would operate from point to point, betting on passenger preference for flying direct to cities of choice rather than to a hub serving a region, where the added annoyance of changing flights to local destinations would have to be endured.

By contrast, the Airbus philosophy was that bigger was better – it would construct a very big aircraft that could carry a large number of passengers from hub to hub, believing that this was where the future of the passenger market lay. Such a plane would enjoy the significant added advantage of much lower fuel consumption per seat/kilometre. The company envisaged a double-deck jumbo aircraft that could carry 550 passengers in a three-class configuration, but with an ultimate capacity of 850 passengers if needed. After intense consultations with major airlines, in 1994 a new standard in aviation was set when Airbus signified its intention to build the biggest commercial airliner ever. The project, at that time referred to as the A3XX, would put Airbus at the forefront of the aircraft manufacturing industry.

Airbus promised unparalleled fuel efficiency, with a target of more passengers per flight and a 15 per cent lower operating cost in fuel burn per seat than the Boeing 747-400. With the budget for the ambitious project set at US$11 billion, Airbus was staking its future on the aircraft. The planned break-even point was 250 aircraft sales, with a price tag of US$280 million apiece; fifty firm orders were needed to get the project off the ground. First to sign on the dotted line was Emirates Airlines, followed soon after by Singapore, Qantas and Virgin Atlantic.

PRODUCTION GOES AHEAD

In 2000, Airbus announced that production would go ahead, and the new aircraft was christened the A380. The main assembly hangar was constructed

Airbus built the
Beluga aircraft
to transport
A380 parts to
Toulouse.
(Benoit
Machefert)

in Toulouse, France, where the parts from the Airbus consortium's
constituent companies in France, Germany, Spain and Britain were to be
assembled into completed aircraft. The main wings were to be built in Britain,
the tail section in Spain, and the fuselage in France and Germany. This
presented the monumental logistical task of transporting all the parts to
Toulouse for assembly. Smaller parts were to be flown to Toulouse in a
specially modified Airbus A300 aircraft called the Beluga, aptly named after
the white whale with its distinctive bulging head. The larger sections, like the
wings and fuselage, however, were too big to fit into the Beluga. Instead, they
were to be shipped by barge and then transported 200km (124 miles) by land
over country roads to the main assembly hanger. Of particular interest was the
passage of the fuselage through the sleepy French village of Levignac, where
only centimetres separated the huge structure from the buildings of the main
street. It was expected that A380 fuselages would creep through the streets of
the village at the rate of one every week once production was in full swing.

In the summer of 2004, as construction of the first aircraft began, rumours
of problems with the wiring started to emerge, suggesting that the assembly
process could be delayed. Airbus cranked up its work rate with round-the-
clock shifts, however, and managed to meet the deadline for the A380's public

Sections of the
A380's massive
fuselage were
transported by
road. (Enrico
Pierobon)

Wing sections pass through a French village at night. (Enrico Pierobon)

unveiling in Toulouse in January 2005. Amazingly, only three years had elapsed since the first metal had been cut for the project in January 2002. Three months later, on a beautiful spring morning on 27 April 2005, the first flight of the A380 took place. The super jumbo, with a crew of two senior test pilots, Claude Lelaie and Jacques Rosay, who jointly captained the aircraft, and four test-flight engineers lifted off in front of 50,000 spectators. The test flight lasted three hours, fifty-four minutes and was a great success.

DELAYS

Behind the euphoric scenes, however, the Airbus production teams were faced with creeping delays in the manufacturing schedule. During the Paris Air Show, in June 2005, the first of a series of production delays was announced, putting back delivery of the first A380 by six months. In the meantime, to satisfy the aviation authorities that the aircraft could be operated safely in all conditions, the rigorous 2,500hr flight certification programme continued.

Another six-month delay was announced in the summer of 2006 at the Farnborough Air Show, much to the disappointment of the launch customers. Airbus was still experiencing a problem with the wiring, as the French- and German-built fuselage sections did not seem to match. Then it was discovered that the two fuselage production teams were using different computer software for their production plans. As a result, it was decided that all plans would comply with the French software program, requiring a revamp of German equipment and manufacturing processes.

A third and final delay, resulting in the project being set back a further year, was announced in the autumn of 2006. Thus, the first production aircraft was delivered two years later than originally intended. The delay meant that Singapore Airlines, the first to fly the A380, did not receive its first aircraft until October 2007. In the meantime, final certification from the regulatory authorities to operate as a commercial airliner had been received in December 2006.

Right: The A380's huge main assembly building in Toulouse. (Rafael Alverez Cacho)

Below: The first ever A380 commercial flight arrives at Sydney in October 2007. (Tim Bowrey)

FIRST COMMERCIAL FLIGHT

In May 2007, the first A380 to be delivered to Singapore Airlines, with manufacturer serial number 003, was rolled out of the production hangar and released for trials prior to delivery in October. The airline inaugurated the first ever A380 commercial flight from Singapore to Sydney, the SQ380, on 25 October 2007.

CHAPTER 3
PRE-DEPARTURE
PREPARATION

DOORS AND ACCESS

Back on the ramp at Heathrow, the pilots undergo a final security check as they enter the aerobridge before boarding the aircraft at main deck door one left (M1L). The three doors of the total of sixteen that are normally used for passenger boarding are M1L, main deck door two left (M2L) and upper deck door one left (U1L). Main deck doors two right (M2R), four left (M4L) and five left (M5L), and the upper deck one right (U1R) are opened for catering uplift and servicing personnel.

The A380's main doors are designed and rated to enable emergency evacuation of the maximum number of 853 passengers and twenty crew members within ninety seconds, using only half the available doors. In March 2006 in Germany, the proving emergency evacuation trial for certification was conducted in a hanger in darkness and was completed successfully. All 873 evacuated the aircraft in seventy-eight seconds by means of only the eight emergency exits and chutes on the right side of the aircraft. All the doors on the left had been blocked to simulate a major hazard, such as a fire. Normally, the sixteen main doors are opened and closed electrically, but in an emergency

are actuated pneumatically to deploy their escape slides. The door slides, excluding the over-wing slides, also double as life rafts and can be detached easily from the aircraft after a ditching in water. With the aircraft settled on the water, passengers and crew can board the inflated slide rafts directly without getting their feet wet.

On the right side of the fuselage are the forward and aft cargo doors, which are hydraulically operated, and a manually operated aft bulk cargo door, which provides access to the hold five cargo area. Gaining access from ground level into the aircraft is also possible via the main avionics hatch located at the left underside of the fuselage, by the nose wheel. This leads to the lower avionics compartment and to a trap door in the cockpit floor. In the cockpit itself, the pilots' two side windows open and can serve as secondary escape routes in an emergency.

FLIGHT CREW PREPARATION

When the flight crew boards the aircraft, the captain meets the cabin crew member in charge of the team. The minimum required cabin crew for the A380 is eighteen, one for each door and an additional crew member for each deck. By now, the cabin crew would be well into the pre-flight preparations of checking the meals and ensuring that all the amenities are loaded. Seats and equipment are also checked, and a security sweep of the cabin is carried out to ensure that nothing untoward has been left on board. The captain briefs the cabin crew member in charge on the details of the flight and, as a meal service is planned, advises that with clear skies forecast when at cruise level, no interruptions are expected.

Next, the flight crew meets the ground engineer, who briefs them on the aircraft serviceability. Engineering staff work hard to ensure the safety and serviceability of the aircraft, and it is a legal requirement that all flights are certified serviceable by the ground engineer prior to departure. Defects in the

Right: On-Board Maintenance Terminal (OMT), used by the ground engineers.

Left: Aircraft being serviced on the apron.

aircraft maintenance 'e-log book' must be attended to before the engineer signs the 'fit for flight' release documents. The engineer accesses the e-log on a computer terminal called the On-Board Maintenance Terminal (OMT), which is located behind the first officer's seat. If time constraints on transits, or unavailability of spares or equipment, prevent repair at line stations, approved minor defects can be left for attention at home base. Such minor problems are entered into a Deferred Defect log, but not before being verified safe by reference to the aircraft's Minimum Equipment List (MEL). The MEL details the minimum equipment needed to operate the flight safely as well as inoperative items that can be deferred for rectification at a later time. Details of any required procedures that relate to the defective items are also included.

On the flight deck, legal aircraft documents, such as the Certificate of Airworthiness (C of A), Certificate of Maintenance (C of M), necessary licences and aircraft insurance are also checked by the flight crew, and verified current and correct.

After the documents have been checked, the On-Board Information System (OIS) is switched on. The OIS electronic documentation is displayed on two On-Board Information Terminals (OITs), screens positioned forward of the pilots' side sticks or joysticks. The OITs display the pages of electronic documents selected by each pilot via a keyboard located beneath a stowable table in front of the pilot. In addition, three back-up laptops containing the flight performance functions of the OIS are available and can be used in the event of failure of an OIT.

Onboard Information Terminal (OIT), used by the pilots to access the aircraft's library, to carry out performance calculations and to communicate with the company.

One of three back-up laptop computers carried in the cockpit in case of failure of an OIT.

The OIS is subdivided into Avionics and Flight Operations sections. In the former are found the e-log books (electronic technical and recording log books) and the Airline Operational Control (AOC), the aircraft and base communication provision. The function of the AOC section is to monitor aircraft systems and gather relevant information for documenting and storing in the archive. The AOC also maintains constant communication with the home base, the information received being used as a flight progress watch.

In the Flight Operations section of the OIS, more commonly known as the Electronic Flight Bag (EFB), is the electronic library of books, or 'e-manuals', such as the Aircraft Performance Manual, Flight Crew Operating Manual, Minimum Equipment List, and Weight and Balance Manual. The Jeppesen aviation terminal and en-route electronic charts are also accessed through this feature.

COCKPIT DISPLAYS

The A380 flight deck has an impressive state-of-the-art 'glass cockpit' display, the earliest forms of which were introduced to commercial aviation in the early eighties with the Airbus A310 and the Boeing 757. Collectively, the 'glass' screens and instrument panels are known as the Control and Display System (CDS), and consist of eight identical liquid-crystal displays (LCDs), two in front of each pilot displaying the flight instruments, and four in an inverted 'T' layout at the centre. The two screens of the OITs, one on each side, bring the total number of displays to ten.

Cockpit Display System (CDS). The OITs are at left and right. Working towards the centre on each side are the Primary Flight Display (PFD) and Navigation Display (ND). The central Engine/Warning Display (EWD) sits above the System Display (SD), which is flanked by Multi-Function Displays (MFDs).

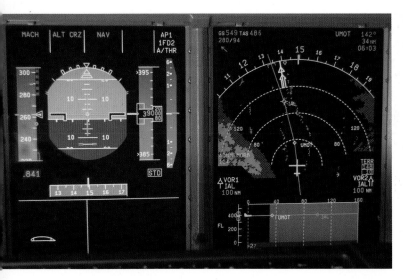

A Primary Flight Display *(left)* and Navigation Display are positioned directly in front of each pilot.

The two LCD screens in front of each pilot, known as Display Units (DUs), are the Primary Flight Display (PFD) and the Navigation Display (ND). Basically, the PFD is used by the pilots as the primary flying instrument. It presents airspeed on the left and, in the centre, the artificial horizon with attitude indication, plus the bank angle above and heading below. On the right are the altitude and vertical speed indicators. At the top of the PFD is the Flight Mode Annunciator (FMA), which displays such supplementary information as autopilot and Flight Director (FD) modes. Colours are used extensively on the PFD: in general, green indicates a captured desired selection, blue a pilot selected target, and magenta a computer generated target.

As its name implies, the ND is used to navigate, or 'guide', the aircraft. It presents the heading at the top with, centre screen, a plan view of the current track, as well as the required track for the flight-plan route ahead. Radio navigation needles (pointers) of the Very High Frequency (VHF) Omni-Range beacons (VORs) can be displayed on the NDs. The radio beacons can be selected from a database stored in the aircraft's computer either automatically or manually. Weather radar returns can also be 'painted' in colour on the NDs, offering a graphic view of the weather ahead in relation to the aircraft's planned track. Green, yellow and red are used to represent the degrees of intensity of the weather, green being the least intense and red the most intense.

A unique feature of the A380's ND is the Vertical Display (VD), which is presented on the lower section of the screen. Plan views of aircraft position have been a common feature on instruments for some time, even on conventional displays, but the VD shows a side elevation of aircraft position. In addition to the projected vertical track of the aircraft, it usefully illustrates the vertical extent of any weather cells. Thus the need for the pilot to estimate

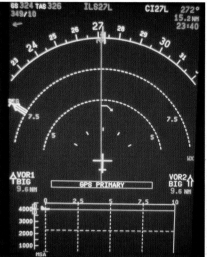

Above: PFD with five-column Flight Mode Annunciator (FMA) at the top. The first column shows engine power; the second and third give the pitch and roll comands of the Flight Director (FD); the fourth is reserved for approach modes; and the fifth indicates autopilot (AP), FD and Autothrust (A/THR) status.

Above right: The Navigation Display shows the track to fly, beacon needles and weather radar return.

Right: Weather radar return displayed on the ND. The Vertical Display (VD) at the bottom provides a vertical profile of the weather.

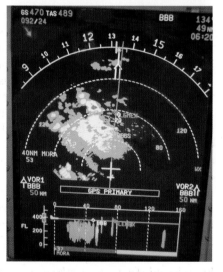

the height of cloud tops and whether or not they can be flown over is eliminated, as the VD display removes the guesswork.

In the forward centre section of the cockpit are two DUs that show the engine instruments and system schematics. The upper DU is called the Engine/Warning Display (EWD) and presents the essential engine instruments on the upper half of the unit, and the malfunction warning messages on the bottom half. The lower DU is called the System Display (SD) and provides the various system schematics of the aircraft when selected. Together they constitute the Electronic Centralized Aircraft Monitoring (ECAM) system. The pilots can call up schematics of the various systems for viewing on the SD using the ECAM Control Panel (ECP) located on the

23

The Electronic Centralized Aircraft Monitoring (ECAM) control panel is below the engine master switches, while the SD is behind the thrust levers.

Below left: Loading the Flight Management System (FMS) computer. Waypoints are displayed on both MFDs.

Below: Keyboard Cursor Control Unit (KCCU) is used by the pilots to interface with the FMS.

centre pedestal, aft of the thrust levers. The ECAM system also functions as an electronic checklist.

Multi-Function Displays (MFDs), situated on both sides of the lower ECAM system display, operate identically and are used independently by the pilot adjacent to each display to interface with the aircraft computers and the Flight Management Computer (FMC). Data are manipulated by means of track-and-ball units and the adjoining Keyboard Cursor Control Units (KCCUs) in a similar manner to the rolling ball and 'qwerty' keyboard of a laptop computer, rather than the typical alpha-numeric keypad found in most other commercial aircraft cockpits.

Heathrow Automatic Terminal Information Service (ATIS) displayed on the MFD, having been received via datalink. It gives wind speed and direction, temperature, altimeter pressure setting and runway in use.

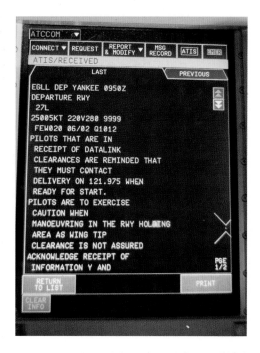

TAKE-OFF PERFORMANCE DATA

After the On-Board Information System (OIS) boot-up, any approved deferred defects allowed by the MEL are entered into the system. Inoperative items that may affect flight operations or degrade aircraft performance are compensated for automatically in performance calculations. If a spoiler is defective and has to be locked down, for example, the calculations would allow for the inoperative item by increasing the required minimum runway lengths for take-off and landing.

Next, the provisional take-off performance figures for the expected runway in use need to be calculated. The Automatic Terminal Information Service (ATIS), which gives information on current local weather conditions and the runway in use, is obtained by typing the airport identification – in this case, London Heathrow's International Civil Aviation Organization (ICAO) four-letter code, EGLL – into the Air Traffic Control (ATC) datalink section on the MFD. Within seconds, the received reply is displayed, giving wind speed and direction, ambient temperature, altimeter pressure setting (the atmospheric pressure at mean sea level), departure runway and runway conditions. The weather conditions and runway data, together with the planned take-off weight of 443.9 tonnes (436.9imp/489.3US tons), are then entered into the Take-Off Performance Application (TOPA) page on the OIT, and the take-off speeds and engine power setting are calculated. Both the pilots accomplish this task independently, comparing the results of their work to make sure that they are correct.

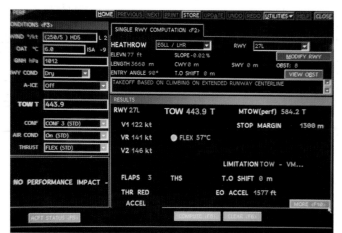

Take-Off Performance Application (TOPA) page displayed on the OIT with the calculated take-off performance numbers.

The take-off speed targets of V1 (122kt), VR (141kt) and V2 (146kt) are displayed on the TOPA page. The V1 speed ('V' stands for velocity) is the go or no-go decision speed, after which the aircraft is committed to the take-off, as the remaining runway length is not guaranteed to be sufficient for stopping. The VR, or rotate, speed is the speed at which sufficient lift is generated by the wings for the aircraft to become airborne. The V2 speed is the safe speed required to ensure obstacle clearance on the climb path if an engine fails during the take-off.

On the A380, power settings are targeted as a percentage of maximum power, unlike earlier aircraft types where power settings are indicated either as a percentage of the maximum rotor speed of the fan compressor (N1) – 93 per cent for example – or as an engine pressure ratio (EPR) – such as 1.58 – representing the ratio of the turbine exhaust pressure to the engine inlet pressure. The planned take-off weight of 443.9 tonnes (436.9imp/489.3US tons) is less than the maximum performance take-off weight of 584.2 tonnes (575.0imp/643.0US tons), so the take-off power required for this particular flight is less than the maximum take-off power. In fact, in normal situations, maximum power is seldom used; reduced power, or 'flex' (flexible) power, as it is referred to on the A380, is usually set to diminish engine wear and prolong engine life.

Although the outside temperature is 6°C, under the 'flex' power concept, the FMC selects a 'flex' temperature of 57°C for the flight from the take-off power derate program. This fools the calculation process into assuming an ambient temperature of 57°C and reducing the engine thrust accordingly (*see* graph opposite). The corresponding calculated thrust target of 88 per cent is then displayed at the top of the thrust indicator on the EWD.

Having completed the TOPA calculation, the two pilots plug in their headsets and select communications to 'on' before beginning any checks. Cockpit lights and seats are adjusted, and paperwork arranged. The EFB is selected, and the required taxi and departure charts are chosen and displayed.

This graph shows the determination of 'flex' thrust for take-off.

Below: On the ground, power is provided to the aircraft by cables plugged into the belly.

Below right: APU exhaust located in the tail section.

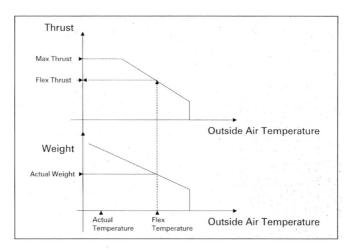

POWER SUPPLY

At this stage, the aircraft's power is supplied by the airport's electrical system through cables plugged into four connectors in the fuselage belly. Before departure, however, this external power source has to be disconnected, whereupon the aircraft's own power supply takes over. This is generated by the Auxiliary Power Unit (APU), an on-board mini gas-turbine engine located in the tail. With ever increasing sensitivity to airport noise, most airports discourage the use of the noisy APUs until a short time before departure. As a precaution, before the APU is started, the fire systems of the APU, engines, cargo holds and landing gear have to be tested by checking the function of the warning bells and lights.

FIRE PROTECTION

Two types of fire detector are used on the aircraft: heat sensors and smoke sensors. Heat sensing loops are employed in the APU, engines and the main landing gear wheel wells; smoke sensing units are fitted in the aircraft compartments, namely the lavatories, cargo bays, crew rest areas and avionics equipment bays.

The engine fire detection loops, two for each engine, are positioned in the cowling areas. They trigger an audio and visual alarm in the cockpit when heat from an engine fire is detected. A red master warning light and an alarm bell are activated, while the respective fire push-button and engine start master switch are also illuminated red. On receipt of an engine fire warning, a two-step 'isolate and extinguish' sequence is initiated. First the crew shuts down the respective engine by closing the thrust lever and selecting the engine start master switch to 'off'. Next, the overhead fire push-button is depressed. This cuts off the fuel supply to the affected engine, isolates its electrics, pneumatics and hydraulics, and arms its two fire extinguisher bottles. These actions are followed by the pilot pressing the 'AGENT 1' switch below the fire push-button to discharge the first fire extinguisher bottle. Immediately, feon gas is discharged into the cowl jacket housing the engine components. If the fire is not extinguished within thirty seconds, the 'AGENT 2' switch is pressed to discharge the second bottle.

Although the main landing gear compartments are fitted with heat sensing detectors, the wheel well bays are not equipped with fire bottles to extinguish a fire. High temperatures detected in the landing gear bays are rarely the result of fire, but more usually are caused when the landing gear is retracted into the bays with overheated brakes. If a high temperature is indicated, the procedure is to extend the landing gear to allow the airflow to cool the hot brakes or to blow out any flames.

In the event of a cargo fire, the crew isolates any airflow into the cargo area

Illuminated engine fire buttons, which would be depressed in the event of a fire warning.

to starve the fire of oxygen and discharges the extinguishing bottles. The forward and aft cargo holds share two extinguishing bottles. The first bottle is fully discharged into the relevant cargo hold and, after an interval, the second is automatically discharged at a metered rate to prolong the smothering effect of the extinguishing agent for a period of four hours. This allows sufficient margin for the crew to divert to a suitable airport for an emergency landing.

In the cabin, two manually activated extinguishing bottles provide fire protection for the main cabin-crew rest area. In the lavatories, individual extinguishing bottles are positioned at the waste bin areas and, in the event of a fire, are discharged automatically by heat sensing units. The fire detection system in the lavatories also monitors for smoke; if detected, this results in a warning being displayed in the cockpit as well as at the Flight Attendant Panels (FAPs) by the doors. If the smoke is the result of fire, the cabin crew fights the flames with hand-held extinguishers.

The avionics equipment compartments are not protected by any extinguishing agents. If smoke is detected in any of the five avionics compartments, the crew action is to open overboard valves to allow the smoke to be sucked out to the atmosphere. The procedure for dealing with this problem requires the aircraft to be landed as soon as possible. In the meantime, the crew will attempt to identify the source of the smoke by systematically switching off each piece of equipment in turn. If the smoke stops, the problem can be isolated by leaving the offending equipment switched off.

THE AUXILIARY POWER UNIT

After testing the fire system, the crew starts the APU. In addition to supplying electric power, the APU provides a pneumatic bleed for the aircraft's air-conditioning system. It takes a couple of minutes to start the

External air-conditioning supply from ground source.

APU, after which the demand for electrical power can be transferred from the four external electrical sources to the two on-board APU generators. At the same time, the air-conditioning supply is also transferred from ground units to the APU. The APU continues to power the electrics and air-conditioning until the four engines have been started, at which time the engine generators, one on each engine, take over the supply to the aircraft's electrical system, while air bled from the engines operates the air-conditioning system. After the engines have begun to power the electrical and air-conditioning systems, the APU is shut down as part of the after-engine-start procedures.

ELECTRICAL SYSTEM

The main aircraft electrical network comprises four AC 115-volt busses supplied by the four engine generators. These, in turn, feed an 'Essential' and an 'Emergency' AC bus, so named because they power the important on-board equipment. Transformer rectifiers tap electricity from these busses and convert AC power to DC. There are two DC busses plus an essential DC bus, which takes care of the vital DC equipment, and an APU DC bus. In the event of all the engine generators failing, four batteries carried in the aircraft cut in to power up the four DC busses. The APU can also be started in flight to supply the failed electrical devices.

In the extreme emergency situation of all four engine generators failing in flight, a propeller driven generator, called the Ram-Air Turbine (RAT), automatically deploys from the underside of the left wing and spins in the airflow to provide AC power to the aircraft. The RAT can supply only 10 per cent of the total power produced by the four engine generators, so its output is channelled solely to equipment that is absolutely essential. The entire electrical system is automatically controlled by two Electrical Network Management Units (ENMUs), which prioritize and distribute the electrical loads to the aircraft systems.

If an engine-driven generator problem occurs, further damage to the generator can be prevented by mechanically disconnecting it from its engine by pressing a button on the overhead panel. A unique feature of the A380 generators is that they do not provide a constant frequency output, as is the case with the generators of earlier aircraft types. Instead, they generate frequencies that vary according to engine speed. This varying frequency is electronically stabilized to 50Hz before being fed into the AC system. The electrical schematic displays of the AC and DC systems can be called up on the SD on the forward lower DU.

AIR-CONDITIONING AND PRESSURIZATION SYSTEM

Air-conditioning for passenger comfort on the ground is provided by compressed air bled from the APU engine. Unlike the closed-loop, gas-type

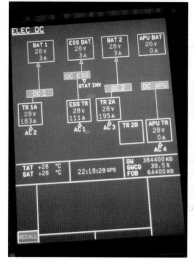

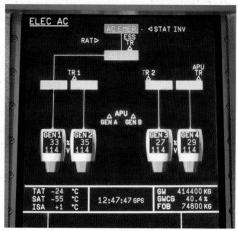

Top left: Ram Air Turbine (RAT) in deployed position. The device provides emergency electrical power by windmilling in the airflow.

Top right: Overhead electrical panel with generator disconnect buttons guarded by red cruciform covers.

Above left: DC electrical system on the System Display (SD).

Above right: AC electrical system on the SD.

air-conditioning system used in our homes, however, the aircraft air-conditioning system is based on Air Cycle Machines (ACMs), which work on the principle that air cools when heat, or work energy, is extracted from it. The compressed air provided by the APU drives each ACM's turbine, which causes the air to expand and cool. This cooled air leaves the turbine at a temperature of -30°C and is mixed with hot trim air before being fed into the

31

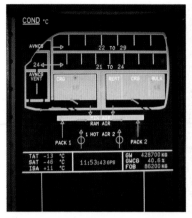
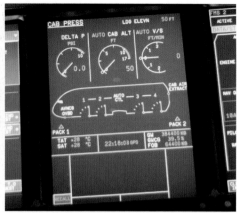

cabins. In flight, the air-conditioning is supplied by compressed air bled from the four main engines, and it may come as a surprise to many that passengers actually breathe air from the engines' inner cores and not air tapped directly from the atmosphere. The ACMs work at maximum rpm on the ground for maximum cooling, but during the cruise they operate at idling mode, as most of the cooling of the tapped engine air is provided by cold ambient air passing through two heat exchangers. The required amount of compressed air tapped from the engines for air-conditioning purposes is reduced by mixing fresh incoming air with reused cabin air. This is accomplished by four primary and nine secondary recirculation fans, and the result is a fuel saving, since less air is tapped from the engine. The air-conditioning system also automatically regulates the amount of incoming fresh air in accordance with the number of passengers on board; that figure is simply entered into the computer by the pilot during the pre-flight procedures. In turn, the cargo compartments are ventilated by air tapped from the main passenger cabins; a separate electric heater provides heating in the aft cargo bay, where live cargo is carried.

The A380 air-conditioning system consists of two air-conditioning units called 'packs', each pack being equipped with two ACMs. In the unlikely event of both packs failing, two emergency ram-air doors can be opened to scoop air to ventilate the aircraft. There are eighteen cabin temperature control zones in the aircraft. Besides being used to keep the aircraft cabin at a comfortable temperature, the air-conditioning supply is employed to pressurize the cabins and cargo holds. The system works on the principle that if the incoming mass of airflow is greater than that leaving the aircraft, the fuselage can be positively pressurized. To maintain the required cabin pressure, a controlled amount of air is exhausted to the atmosphere by four regulated outflow valves in the underside of the fuselage, two forward and two aft. Normally, the aircraft cabin is regulated at a comfortable pressure equivalent to an altitude of about 6,000ft and is prevented from exceeding an equivalent altitude of 7,500ft.

The air-conditioning and pressurization system schematics can be displayed

Right: ECAM control panel with buttons for the various aircraft systems.

Far left: Air-conditioning schematic on the SD.

Left: Aircraft pressurization system.

Right: Engine instruments displaying, from the top, rotation speed of the N2 and N3 compressors; fuel flow; oil quantity, temperature and pressure; vibration of the three spools; and lastly nacelle temperature on the SD.

Below: Flight control surfaces displayed diagramatically on the SD.

Below right: Bleed system schematic selected on the SD.

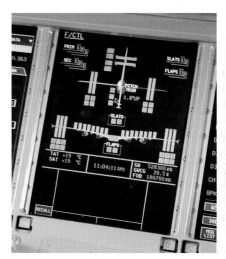

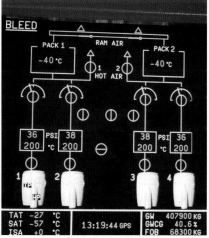

on the lower SD by selecting the appropriate buttons on the ECAM Control Panel (ECP). Examples of other schematics that can be displayed on the SD are engines, flight controls, pneumatics, hydraulics, doors, wheels, electrics and fuel.

Throughout the flight, the entire operation of the pressurization system, from engine start to engine shut-down, is automatically managed by four pressurization controllers; no pilot input is required. Automatic pressurization begins at the start of the take-off, a positive pressure differential between the cabin interior and the outside atmosphere being created as soon as the aircraft lifts off. The cabin 'altitude' immediately starts to climb at about 300ft/min, a much slower rate than the aircraft itself, to a targeted cabin altitude that depends on the final cruising altitude of the aircraft. Skybird 380 will be cruising at flight level (FL) 370, or 37,000ft, requiring a matching target cabin altitude of 6,000ft. As the aircraft climbs above 10,000ft, the internal cabin pressure is sufficiently positive to prevent anyone from forcing any of the aircraft's plug-type doors open. On descent, the cabin altitude descends at a regulated rate so that it matches the destination airport altitude on landing. On the odd occasion, such as landing at Mexico City, the cabin altitude would actually ascend, in that particular case to 7,400ft, the elevation of the airport. This is automatically provided by the computer's navigation database.

In the event of failure of the pressurization system's automatic mode, a manual back-up mode is available. 'Manual' is a misnomer, however, as the back-up mode is semi-automatic. It requires the pilot to select the desired altitudes for cruise and landing, and to initiate the climb or descent of the cabin altitude by pressing a button. The rate of cabin climb or descent to the targeted altitude is then controlled automatically.

RAMP ACTIVITY

On the flight deck of Skybird 380, preparations for departure continue. Before the first officer begins the external walk-around, the cockpit safety checks are carried out. These include checking the quantity of windshield rain-repellent fluid, and the levels of the engine oil, hydraulic fluid and emergency oxygen supply. Having donned a high-visibility yellow tabard, a mandatory requirement for apron movement, the first officer proceeds down the side steps to the ramp. As mentioned, by now the ground engineer would have completed a thorough visual inspection of the aircraft and certified it as airworthy, but the first officer's walk-around is an essential last check to ensure that all is well. The aircraft's exterior is given a quick inspection to ensure that all the requisite 'bits and pieces' are in place, that there is no recent skin damage from service trucks or other vehicles, and that such items as the landing gear lock pins have been removed and that no overnight protective covers have been left installed.

As the first officer undertakes the ramp inspection, there is a hive of activity

Refuelling trucks pump kerosene into the aircraft's tanks from underground hydrants.

around the aircraft. Catering trucks, specially modified for the A380, load the galleys on the main and upper decks. All the cargo doors are open; while smaller cargo items are loaded into the bulk cargo bay, high-loaders feed containers into the forward and aft main cargo compartments. Once aboard, the containers are moved on electrically driven wheels that manoeuvre them into their respective positions. A toilet truck, known as a 'honey wagon', discharges the contents of the four toilet waste tanks and recharges them with sanitized 'blue' water. Meanwhile, another truck fills the four water reservoirs with fresh drinking water.

The aircraft is also being refuelled by two bowsers, one on each side, that are connected to valves beneath the left and right wings. With each truck being capable of pumping kerosene at a rate of up to 3,000 litres/min (660imp/790US gal/min) into the aircraft tanks from underground hydrants, the refuelling process takes about half an hour. Refuelling the A380 is a fully automatic process: the ground engineer is only required to enter the amount of fuel for the flight on the refuelling panel, located in the aircraft's underbelly, aft of the left gear, and then to press the 'auto-start' button. Load controllers at the Dubai home base would already have sent to the A380's computer by satellite datalink the aircraft's Zero Fuel Weight Centre of Gravity (ZFWCG). ZFW is a sum of all weights for the flight, excluding fuel. The expected cargo and passenger load figures determine the ZFWCG, which in turn will determine the distribution of the fuel. The calculated final load and fuel distribution, therefore, ensure a properly trimmed and balanced aircraft for the critical take-off phase.

FUEL SYSTEM AND WIRING

All fuel on the A380 is carried in tanks in the wings, with the exception of a small trim tank in the horizontal stabilizer (movable tailplane) at the rear of the aircraft. A further consideration, therefore, is the effect of fuel load on the wing structure, so fuel distribution is also determined by whether the aircraft is on the ground or in the air. If the aircraft is on the ground, the fuel is distributed more towards the centre, to the tanks nearest the landing gear, rather than the outer wing tanks, thus reducing the downward bending moment on the outboard wing. Soon after take-off, however, the fuel is redistributed to the outer wing tanks to spread the weight of the fuel along the length of the wing, countering the upward bending moment of the wing caused by aerodynamic lift. Two Fuel Quantity and Management System (FQMS) computers control fuel distribution during refuelling and in all phases of the flight. In addition, when airborne, the FQMS moves fuel forward from the horizontal stabilizer trim tank to maintain an optimum flying CG, using its CG transfer system.

On the A380, there are eleven tanks in total, ten in the wings plus the trim tank in the horizontal stabilizer. Six of the wing tanks and the trim tank are 'storage' tanks, while the remaining four are 'feed' tanks, each supplying fuel to its respective engine. Fuel is transferred from the storage tanks to the feed tanks, each of the latter having two boost pumps to supply fuel to its engine. Strictly speaking, the storage tanks are 'transfer' tanks, as fuel moves constantly from them to the feed tanks and between them for balancing purposes. The feed tanks are further subdivided into smaller 'collector' tanks, each holding about 1,500kg (3,000lb) of fuel, to ensure that the boost pumps remain submerged in the fuel at all aircraft attitudes, especially if fuel levels are low when the aircraft nose pitches up during take-off or a go-around. The collector tanks prevent the fuel from rushing rearwards, ensuring that the boost pumps do not run dry and that positive fuel feed is maintained to the engines at all times. In total, there are twenty-two pumps in the system, fourteen transfer pumps and eight boost pumps.

The total fuel capacity of the A380 is approximately 254 tonnes (250.0imp/280.0US tons), depending on the fuel's specific gravity at the time. The FQMS computers constantly monitor the fuel used by the four

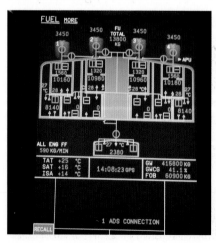

Fuel page selected on the SD, showing the arrangement of the tanks, valves (circles) and pumps (square boxes).

engines and the quantity remaining in the tanks; by comparing these two figures, they are capable of detecting a fuel leak. If a large discrepancy is sensed, a warning of a possible leak is triggered in the cockpit by the electronic warning system, and the pilots carry out the electronic checklist procedure displayed on the EWD. Crew actions are to isolate the leaking tank and to transfer as much fuel from it to other tanks as quickly as possible.

In the event of an emergency requiring a premature landing, fuel can be dumped to reduce the aircraft's weight to below its maximum landing weight of 390 tonnes (383.9imp/430.0US tons). In a dire emergency, the aircraft is safe to land in an overweight condition, but the high stresses that the airframe is likely to suffer make this highly undesirable. Fuel dumping is fully automatic; all the crew needs to do is enter the desired landing weight into the computer and push the fuel jettison button. The fuel dumping system employs all the integral transfer pumps to channel fuel to two overboard dumping nozzles, located at the trailing edge of each wing, between the engine pairs. It is capable of dumping fuel at a rate of 2.5 tonnes/min (2.5imp/2.8US tons/min). Only fuel from the transfer tanks can be dumped overboard; it cannot be jettisoned from the feed tanks. The latter have a maximum total capacity of 80 tonnes (78.7imp/88.2US tons) of fuel. If a problem arises just after take-off requiring an immediate landing, at normal operating loads, and with 80 tonnes in the feed tanks, the aircraft is likely to be landing above the recommended maximum landing weight of 390 tonnes.

The wiring of the A380 incorporates the latest in electronic data transfer technology, information being exchanged through an Avionic Full Duplex (AFDX) network system, which is based on aviation-adapted ethernet technology, rather than the traditional thirty-year-old Aircraft Data Network (ADN) wiring system found on older aircraft. AFDX, developed by Airbus for the A380, utilizes sophisticated 'switches' that process and channel multi, high-speed transmissions of data throughout the system without the risk of transmission 'collisions'. As a result, the system requires significantly less

Fuel jettison nozzle. The aircraft is equipped with one on the trailing edge of each wing.

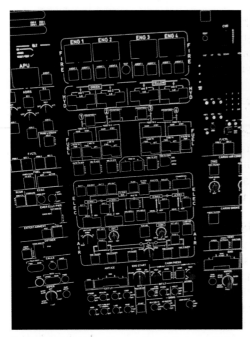

Above: The three Air Data Inertial Reference System (ADIRS) switches on the overhead panel.

Left: 'Dark' panel concept means that all is normal when no coloured lights are illuminated.

wiring with fewer wiring runs – the absence of cumbersome and heavy wiring between components reduces weight. Seven Core Processor Input and Output Modules (CPIOMs) process transmissions between each of the seven main avionics subsystems, namely, air-conditioning, bleed air, cockpit, communication, electrical, fuel and landing gear.

AIR DATA INERTIAL REFERENCE SYSTEM

While the first officer carries out the walk-around, a systematic scan of all the cockpit panels is conducted by the captain. The scan begins at the overhead panels, moves down to the forward panels, and then progresses to the centre and side consoles, all switches and buttons being placed in their respective positions in turn. A 'dark' panel philosophy is practised on the A380, whereby the absence of lights means that all is normal, while an illuminated button signifies a forgotten item or a malfunction warning. As part of the scan, the all-important Air Data Inertial Reference System (ADIRS) selectors are turned on.

The ADIRS functions as two systems in one, namely an Air Data System and an Inertial Reference System (IRS). Using pressure-based information, the former computes airspeed and altitude for display on the aircraft's instruments and computers; laser gyros are employed by the latter to sense aircraft attitude and acceleration, the data being computed mathematically for navigational use. The attitude information is also used for the artificial horizon instruments on the PFDs, and the Auto Flight and Flight Director

(FD) systems. The IRS needs a geographical reference as a starting point to begin navigating, however, and this is provided by the aircraft's position being automatically captured from the Global Positioning System (GPS) when the ADIRS is switched on; no pilot input is required.

NAVIGATION SYSTEM

The forerunner of the laser gyro-equipped IRS was the Inertial Navigation System (INS), which was developed for the Apollo space missions and was made famous by the moon landing in 1969. INS revolutionized navigation practices, as it operated independently of ground-station sources. When introduced into civil aviation in the early seventies, it made the on-board flight navigator redundant.

Prior to the introduction of INS, navigation on airways was accomplished by the pilot steering the aircraft from one radio beacon to another along the airway. These navigational beacons, such as the VORs and the slightly longer-range Non-Directional Beacons (NDBs), were limited in range, and navigation in remote areas without such ground radio beacons for guidance was conducted by a flight navigator plotting the aircraft's position on a chart from other sources. The navigator used a method called Dead Reckoning (DR), whereby a rough estimate of position was continuously plotted on a chart. Using the estimated position, the navigator would select suitable navigation aids to plot the position accurately and would advise the pilot to make adjustments to the aircraft heading to maintain track. Over such featureless areas as the Sahara desert and the great oceans, where ground-based aids were not available, at night an astro (star) shot could be taken with a special sextant that protruded from the top of the fuselage to obtain a celestial fix of position.

Later, Long-Range Navigation (LORAN) was introduced. This allowed an aircraft's position to be plotted by the intersection of low-frequency radio transmissions from at least two ground stations. Also used was onboard Doppler radar, which could measure ground speed and drift by comparing the shift between signals transmitted from the aircraft and returns received from the ground. It could be inaccurate when flying over oceans with calm seas, however, owing to the poor signal returns received from the flat surface.

These navigation tools were followed by the introduction of INS, with its mechanical gyros, in the early seventies and then, in the eighties, by the more accurate IRS, with its non-moving laser gyros. As with any gyro system, however, laser gyros are prone to drift, and small inaccuracies can occur over time. To correct for gyro drift, in-range ground-based Distance Measuring Equipment (DME) radio beacons were used during flight to update navigation accuracy. Later, with the release of the US military Global Positioning System (GPS) satellites for civilian use, the accuracy and integrity of IRS navigation was greatly enhanced when GPS was employed to update it. GPS uses line-of-sight satellites to plot an exact position by triangulation, to an accuracy of a few feet. In fact, on the A380, the back-up in the event of air-pressure altimeter failure is a GPS altimeter.

The IRS, with GPS updating, provides highly accurate navigation and allows routings to be flown precisely. To accommodate flights using such sophisticated navigation technology, a new standard of route navigation with reduced tolerances, known as Area Navigation (RNAV), was introduced for suitably equipped aircraft. The higher standard of accuracy resulted in reduced separation on airways. This, in turn, allowed better air traffic management and increased traffic loads. To ensure safe separation between aircraft on RNAV-designated routes, a required accuracy of aircraft navigational performance was introduced, called the Required Navigation Performance (RNP). Aircraft operating under RNAV conditions on airway routings, for example, require RNP 5, whereby any navigational error must be less than 5nm. The more critical airport terminal areas require RNP 1, where any navigational error must be less than 1nm.

GPS-assisted navigation has proved to be so accurate that RNAV approaches have been approved, allowing aircraft to navigate in both the horizontal and vertical profile down to a minimum height of 250ft above the landing runway. Thus RNAV approaches with GPS monitoring, without any reliance on ground-based radio equipment, can guide an aircraft to short final for landing.

The Global Navigation Satellite System (GNSS), at present GNSS-1, is the generic term used for satellite navigation systems that eventually will upgrade to GNSS-2 by encompassing the United States' Navstar GPS, the Russian Glonass, the European Galileo and the Chinese Compass systems for world-wide navigation and precision approach applications. For precision approaches, satellite signals are augmented by Satellite Based Augmentation Systems (SBAS) and Ground Based Augmentation Systems (GBAS), which provide error corrections for greater accuracy. The system in the USA, known as the Wide Area Augmentation System (WAAS), is fully operational and is certified down to a minimum height of 200ft. Local Area Augmentation Systems (LAAS) are being developed for GNSS-2, whereby local ground augmentation units at airports worldwide will be able to provide highly accurate Localizer (runway centreline) Performance with Vertical Guidance (LPV) down to very low minimum heights, leading eventually to fully automatic landings.

Navigational Programming

Having completed the pre-flight panel scan, the captain begins the navigational programming of the Flight Management System (FMS) computer by keying in the flight plan details. The Flight Management Computer (FMC) has a navigation database that helps the pilots to manage the flight in the safest and most efficient manner. The database is updated periodically with the latest routing information and aircraft performance data. The pilots use the system to plan the flight with the aid of the KCCUs.

Programming the Flight Management System (FMS) by means of the Keyboard and Cursor Control Unit (KCCU).

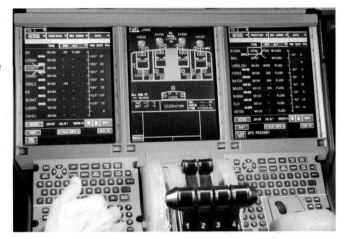

First, the flight number and ICAO four-letter designators for the departure and arrival airports – EGLL (Heathrow) and OMDB (Dubai) – are entered on the Initialization (INIT) page. Then a route request is sent via ACARS datalink to the Dubai home base flight control centre; within seconds the company sends back the selected filed flight-plan routing, which is displayed, checked and accepted by the captain. A total forecast wind model, consisting of four levels of winds and ambient temperatures along the planned flight route, is also datalinked to the aircraft FMS. This allows a more accurate estimate of en-route and arrival times, and fuel predictions.

The planned routing can be programmed in the FMS in three ways. First, as already described, the routing can be downloaded from home base via datalink. If the datalink fails, however, the pilot can search the FMC navigation database for a similar, standard pre-programmed routing and select that for use. Finally, if the required standard routing is not available in the navigation database, a route can be built up 'manually' by diligently selecting the required airways from point to point, in this case the start point of the first airway near London to the end point of the last airway at Dubai. Before any programmed routing is activated, it is essential to cross-check the total indicated FMS mileage with the total distance of the route from the printed flight plan. This is a quick and easy way of confirming the accuracy of the programmed route. A more detailed check of the waypoints en route is usually conducted during the unhurried cruise phase of the flight.

After entering the planned airway routing into the FMS, the captain selects the London departure routing for the first portion of the flight. All busy airports have standard routings that lead an aircraft from the take-off runway to a point aloft where it can join an airway to its destination, very much like a car following a route on a minor road to join a major highway. These routings are called Standard Instrument Departures (SIDs). The filed flight-plan SID routing that directs Skybird 380 to the first en-route airway is 'Detling 2 Golf', and the captain inputs 'DET 2G' into the FMS. The SID is

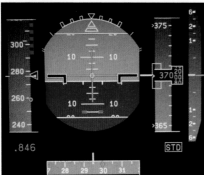

Above: Central Auto Flight System (AFS) panel is flanked by panels for the Electronic Flight Instrument Systems (EFISs).

Left: Flight Director (FD) bars on the Primary Flight Display (PFD). The two green bars cross in the centre of the display, the vertical 'roll' bar providing lateral direction, and the horizontal 'pitch' bar showing the vertical profile to fly.

shown on the ND as a green line, and the lateral and vertical paths of the route are checked on the Flight Plan page on the MFD. As part of the checks, the captain works through the SID from waypoint to waypoint, cross-checking each stage with the Jeppesen chart of the published DET 2G SID, which is displayed on the side OIT screen.

Jeppesen charts depict taxiways, runways, departure and approach paths, terminal routings and en-route airways, together with waypoints, radio beacons, airports, and minimum safe altitudes (MSAs) superimposed on a light background map of terrain. These charts had their humble beginnings in the early thirties, when Elrey Borge Jeppesen, a US mail pilot, made useful notes in a 'little black book' to help him find his way into and out of the many airports he visited. At first, he kept the information solely for his own use, but later he began sharing it with fellow pilots. Eventually, this led to him publishing charts for sale. Today maps and charts produced by the Jeppesen Company, based in Colorado, are the most widely used in aviation. Other commonly used aviation maps are published by AERAD in the UK, LIDO in Germany and EAG in Sweden among others.

After completing the FMS programming, the captain turns his attention to the Flight Control Unit (FCU) panel located on the glare shield above the forward centre instrument display. The FCU panel consists of the Auto Flight System (AFS) control panel in the middle with an Electronic Flight Instrument System (EFIS) panel on each side, one for each pilot. The captain turns on the Flight Director (FD) by pressing the FD button and sets the first 'climb limit' altitude of 6,000ft, as stipulated by the SID in the AFS altitude window. When the FD is switched on, it is represented by two green bars, a horizontal 'pitch' bar and a vertical 'roll' bar, displayed on the PFD. When flying the aircraft as directed by the flight computers, the horizontal bar gives 'up and down' guidance in the vertical plane, and the vertical bar gives 'turning' guidance in the horizontal plane. The FD bars can be followed by the pilot or, if connected, by the autopilot.

AUTO FLIGHT SYSTEM

The AFS panel has speed, heading, altitude and vertical speed windows. When a desired flight selection is made by the pilot on the AFS, the FD bars move in response to commands from the FD computer. The pilot simply 'flies' the bars crossed in the centre of the PFD to achieve the desired flight profile. If the autopilot is activated, it flies the FD targets as set by the pilot on the AFS. As the FD is usually linked to the FMS computer, it is the FMS that provides the guidance information to the FD bars.

On the AFS control panel, below the FD button, are two buttons labelled 'AP1' and 'AP2', which activate the A380's two autopilots. Only one autopilot is used at a time, except when on an automatic landing, when both systems are activated as a precaution against one failing prior to touchdown. Beneath the FD and AP buttons is the Auto Thrust ('A/THR') button.

The pilot selects the waypoint constraints on the EFIS panel. The constraints are published altitude or speed restrictions at points on the SID

The AFS panel. On the left is the speed and heading selector. In the centre are the Flight Director ('FD'), autopilot ('AP1', 'AP2') and Auto Thrust ('A/THR') buttons. On the right is the altitude selector.

flight profile with which the pilots are required to comply. Pressing the constraints button displays the restrictions on the ND as a visual reminder. Also on the EFIS, the VOR radio beacon needles, and the Traffic Collision and Avoidance System (TCAS) are selected to 'on'. The TCAS system senses conflicting air traffic, calculates its trajectory and commands the autopilot (if switched on) to react accordingly to avoid collision. The weather radar selector is left off, as the radar antenna's powerful transmissions can be injurious to the health of personnel on the ramp; it is not switched on to display weather returns until the aircraft lines up on the runway.

FLIGHT CREW DUTIES

On returning from the walk-around, the first officer completes the pre-flight scan checks of the panels at the centre and right side of the cockpit, then cross-checks the FMS data entered by the captain on the MFD. Having confirmed that the FMS programming is correct, the co-pilot joins the captain in the final cockpit preparation checks. Normally, the two pilots will take turns in flying the aircraft. When doing so, the crew member is officially designated 'Pilot Flying' (PF); the other, as the supporting pilot, is known as 'Pilot Not Flying' (PNF). The process of sharing the flying with, for example, one flying out to a destination and the other flying back, enables both pilots to maintain practice and allows the first officer to gain experience that eventually will lead to command.

The duties of the PF and PNF are clearly defined. The former flies the aircraft at all times, and calls for the selection of buttons, levers and computer inputs. The PNF actions those commands, including the recalling and reading of the appropriate checklists, and undertakes radio communications with ATC. The PNF is also a 'clerk' of sorts in the cockpit, being responsible for all the paperwork and record keeping.

On this particular flight, the captain makes the decision to be the designated PF and, in that role, conducts the pre-flight briefing, beginning with the serviceability of the aircraft. Any deferred items entered into the maintenance e-log are highlighted and the accompanying procedures revised. Then the departure airport NOTAMS are reviewed, any taxiway closures, equipment failures or other concerns being noted. Next, the captain briefs the 'game plan' of the flight's departure, including the taxi route to the runway and the details of the expected SID to be flown. Any abnormal or emergency procedures pertinent to the critical take-off stage are discussed. Also covered are the procedures for an engine failure before or soon after V1. If an engine failure occurs before V1, the captain will reject the take-off and stop the aircraft; if it happens after V1, the captain will continue the take-off. Some airports have high ground in the vicinity of the take-off path; if an engine fails, the aircraft's climb ability will be compromised and it may not be able to clear such height obstructions. In such cases, special published procedures for an engine-out escape route avoiding the high terrain are also reviewed.

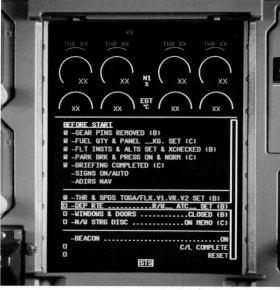

Above: ATC clearance being requested in typed form via datalink instead of by voice transmission.

Right: Before Start checklist is called up on the Engine/Warning Display (EWD). When 'ticked', the blue entries change colour to green, signifying completion.

These engine-failure routings are found in the FMS database and are available for quick retrieval at the click of a button if the need arises.

After the captain's briefing, the requested clearance for the departure routing is transmitted via datalink, using the MFD, to ATC centre at Heathrow Delivery. The datalink reply with the clearance is received almost immediately, being printed, verified and accepted. Until recently, voice radio communication was the only means of requesting departure clearances, but now, with datalink, these clearances are received in a printed format. This reduces the likelihood of miscommunication or a mistake, improving safety. The clearance received by Skybird 380 consists of the runway in use, 27L (left); the SID (Detling 2G); the calculated take-off time (CTOT) or departure 'slot' time of 1140Z (Zulu: Greenwich Mean Time or GMT); and the 'squawk' code number 2211. The 'squawk' number is transmitted by the aircraft's transponder to ATC radar for identification purposes. It produces a display on the air traffic controller's radar screen in the form of a data label showing the aircraft's call sign, altitude, speed and track.

Once the ATC clearance has been verified, the captain calls for the Before Start checklist, which is selected by the first officer as PNF and is displayed on the EWD on the upper centre screen. The PNF reads and 'ticks off' the items on the checklist using the cursor button, very much like a computer mouse, the completed 'challenge' statements changing from blue to green. Some tasks in the checklist are 'closed loop', in that the process is automatically sensed, the colour changing to green when an action is taken. One example is when the anti-collision beacon lights are switched on, whereupon the checklist confirms that the action has been completed by the colour changing automatically to green. As a matter of practice, on

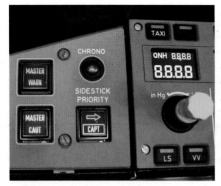

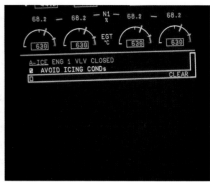

The master caution and warning lights illuminate when an abnormality is sensed. This is accompanied by an Electronic Centralized Aircraft Monitoring (ECAM) message on the Engine/Warning Display (EWD).

When the crew carries out the action specified by an ECAM message, the line changes colour to white to indicate completion.

completion of every checklist, the first officer states, 'Checklist complete.' The captain, glancing at the display to verify that no blues remain, responds with 'Check.'

ELECTRONIC CENTRALIZED AIRCRAFT MONITORING

The advent of sophisticated electronics in aircraft allowed the development of the ECAM system, including a Flight Warning System (FWS), to act as a monitoring and warning computer system for the aircraft. Any system abnormality detected is displayed as an ECAM message on the upper EWD and lower SD centre screens. The crew is alerted to malfunctions by the sound of a warning chime and a master warning or caution light on the glare-shield panel. An ECAM message is displayed together with the appropriate checklist, giving the correct actions to be taken to deal with the situation. As the PNF carries out and 'ticks off' the corrective actions, the checklist entries change from blue to white, signifying action completed.

After the required ECAM actions have been completed, the pilots will consider their options for remedying the abnormality. If this is not possible, a reminder message of the malfunction appears in the form of an aircraft situation report on the ECAM Status page for reference and review. Any new aircraft status that can cause degradation of performance will require the pilot to enter the condition in the OIS. The abnormality is then factored into the approach and landing calculations, as the performance of the aircraft might be affected.

The ECAM also provides the normal electronic checklists, namely Before Start, After Start, Before Take-Off, After Take-Off, Descend, Approach,

Landing, After Landing, Shut Down and Terminating. In the past, the management and monitoring of the aircraft systems, and the reading of paper checklists, was carried out by a third crew member, the knowledgeable and skilled flight engineer. Sadly, just as the advent of the INS hastened the demise of the flight navigator, so the arrival of the ECAM system saw the departure of the flight engineer. Before the flight navigator, it was the radio officer who became redundant, when improved radios were introduced and it was no longer necessary to wind out long trailing antenna wires for the antiquated equipment. The cockpit crew complement of days gone by has dwindled from five to the two pilots. Who knows, perhaps before long, we may lose another pilot – or perhaps both!

WEIGHT AND BALANCE

By now, the ground engineers have finished refuelling the aircraft and, without crew involvement, the final fuel load for the aircraft's weight and balance calculations is automatically datalinked to load masters at the home base in Dubai. The completed load sheet, with the weight and balance details, is sent directly back to the aircraft, via the ACARS datalink, for printing and final checking by the flight crew. The load sheet contains the Take-Off Weight (TOW) and the Zero Fuel Weight (ZFW), including the passenger and cargo loads, in kilograms. The ZFW Centre of Gravity (ZFWCG), the TOW Centre of Gravity (TOWCG) and the take-off horizontal stabilizer trim setting are all expressed as percentages of the Mean Aerodynamic Chord (MAC) of the wing – the average length of the fore-and-aft cross-section through the tapered wing. A ZFWCG of 35 per cent indicates that the CG of the aircraft without fuel acts through a point at 35 per cent of the length of the wing's mean chord.

The aircraft's CG is assumed to act through a single point, the position of which varies fore and aft, within limits, depending on the load distribution. Since the CG is roughly in the middle of the aircraft, in line with the wings, the MAC is used like a measuring stick. The exact longitudinal position of the CG is stated as the percentage of the length from the forward end of the MAC to the CG position divided by the total length of the MAC.

Usually the loading of fuel and payload is arranged to ensure that the TOWCG is near its optimum position of 39.5 per cent of MAC. The loadmaster also directs the aircraft loading to ensure that the ZFWCG results in balanced flight for all payloads in the unlikely event of the tanks running dry. When the ZFWCG is sent by the loadmasters to the aircraft computers prior to refuelling, the fuel computers distribute the fuel accordingly to achieve the TOWCG of 39.5 per cent of MAC.

If any last-minute changes occur, owing to a shift in cargo or passenger loading, the new ZFWCG has to be re-entered into the FMS computer. Any change to the optimum TOWCG is resolved by transferring fuel to rebalance the aircraft and to return the CG to the ideal position. Recovery of the

The load and balance sheet is sent to the aircraft via datalink and printed out for verification.

aircraft's optimum TOWCG is easily achieved by pressing the 'Auto Ground Transfer' switch on the cockpit overhead panel. This causes fuel to flow automatically to or from the stabilizer trim tank to obtain the 39.5 per cent target. It is essential that the aircraft is always perfectly balanced for take-off, as it may not be flyable in an extreme unbalanced condition. The TOWCG also influences the horizontal stabilizer trim, which is set to balance the aircraft in the first airborne moments after take-off. Unlike other aircraft, where the stabilizer trim is set as a unit of nose-up trim, the A380 stabilizer is set with reference to the TOWCG.

The final load and balance sheet is datalinked to the aircraft prior to departure. The flight crew prints out the load sheet, checking and entering the final loads into the FMS. They re-enter the data into their OIS computers for the final recalculation of take-off speeds and power required. Then the pilots cross-check the calculations; if all is correct, they enter the take-off speeds and power setting into the FMS on the MFD.

CHAPTER 4
ENGINE START
AND TAXI

At 1100Z, on the scheduled departure time for Skybird 380's flight to Dubai, all the doors are closed and the flight is ready to depart, but the slot time of 1140Z means a delay of another fifteen minutes or so before the push back. The first officer contacts Heathrow Clearance Delivery by radio with a request that a 'ready message' be sent to Eurocontrol in the hope that the slot time may be improved.

F/O: 'Heathrow Delivery, Skybird 380, clearance by datalink, bay number three zero one, information Yankee, QNH [the local area altimeter pressure setting] one zero one two. We are fully ready.'

Clearance Delivery: 'Skybird 380, your slot time is one one four zero zulu. I will send a ready message.'

A minute later, the good news of an improved departure slot is received and an immediate start clearance is given.

Clearance Delivery: 'Skybird 380, your new slot is one one two one. Clear to start. Call one two one seven for push. Good-day.'

F/O: 'Roger, one two one seven for push. Thank you, Skybird 380.'

As the engines are not started until the aircraft has been pushed back, the first officer contacts Heathrow Ground immediately and requests push back.

F/O: 'Afternoon Heathrow Ground, Skybird 380 at stand three zero one, request push.'

Ground: 'Afternoon Skybird 380, clear push, face east.'

The first officer reads back the clearance and turns his attention to the last items on the Before Start checklist as the captain calls for it to be completed. Then the captain switches on the flashing red anti-collision beacons as an

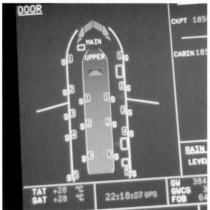

Above: Taxi video shows two views, one from the top of the tail and the other from the belly of the aircraft. The right-hand display shows the Onboard Airport Navigation System (OANS) airport moving map.

Left: The Door System Display. The letter 'S' by each door indicates that its escape slide is armed and ready for deployment in an emergency.

indication to those on the ground that the engines are about to start; the beacons will remain on until the engines are shut down on arrival. Both crew members select the External and Taxiing Aid Camera System (ETACS) switch to 'on', and the Primary Flight Display (PFD) becomes a TV screen displaying a view of the nose-wheel area at the top and, in the centre, a bird's-eye view of the aircraft from the top of the vertical tail fin, 24m (80ft) from the ground. The Navigation Display (ND) is also selected to a ground-map mode called the On-Board Airport Navigation System (OANS) and displays a Global Positioning System (GPS) moving map of the airport with all the taxiway designations clearly shown, very much like the road maps displayed by car GPS systems.

With the Before Start checklist completed, the captain uses the aircraft's intercom to relay the Air Traffic Control (ATC) push-back instructions to the ground engineer, releasing the brakes on the engineer's command. A mighty roar is heard as the push-back tractor starts to push the massive aircraft backwards using a bar attached to the nose gear. To allow the nose gear to swivel freely during the push back, the ground crew would have inserted a

The engine start switch (centre of photo) on the overhead panel arms the automatic engine start sequence when selected to 'IGN START'.

steering bypass pin to isolate the aircraft's hydraulics from the nose-wheel steering system. On sensing movement of the aircraft as the push back begins, members of the cabin crew select the doors to 'arm' ready for emergency deployment. The schematic on the Door System Display shows the letter 'S' next to each door, indicating that the slides have been armed for emergency deployment.

ENGINE START

After receiving a clearance from the ground engineer, the captain begins the engine start procedure, starting the number-three and number-four engines on the right wing simultaneously. These engines are started first because their hydraulic pumps pressurize the 'Yellow' hydraulic system, which powers the body gear steering. Wheels on the main body gear move to help steer the aircraft on the ground, an especially useful feature when manoeuvring in restricted areas. The captain rotates the start switch to 'IGN START' (Ignition Start) and the engine start sequence is armed for a fully automatic start. Air pressure is cut to the air-conditioning packs, as every ounce of air bled from the Auxiliary Power Unit (APU) is required to drive the pneumatic starter unit, which turns the compressors of the giant engines. The passengers may notice a reduction in airflow in the cabins as the air-conditioning packs shut down.

The captain selects the fuel master switches for the number-three and number-four engines to 'on', and the start valves open to supply compressed air to turn each starter unit. The starter unit drives the N3 compressor spool of the three-spool Rolls-Royce Trent 970 engine through a series of gears. The compressors are denoted N1 for the fan rotors, N2 for the mid-compressor and N3 for the high-pressure compressor. Air drawn through the engine by the N3 compressor drives turbines that rotate the N2 and N1 compressors by means of shafts. As sufficient air flows into the combustion chambers, to the rear of the compressors, fuel is injected and the fuel/air

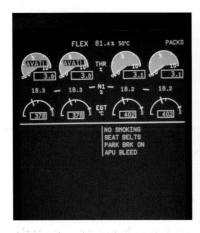

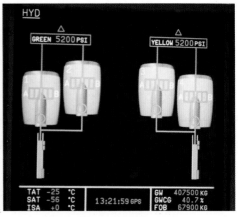

On completion of a successful start, the word 'AVAIL' is displayed on the engine thrust indicator.

Hydraulic system display. Both systems, 'Green' and 'Yellow', show 5,200psi (359 bar) pressure from the eight engine pumps (square boxes labelled 'A' and 'B').

mixture is fired by one of two sets of igniters, which function like a car engine's spark plugs. The hot exhaust gases expelled from the combustion chambers drive the engine turbines that, in turn, accelerate the compressors until a self-sustaining rotation speed is reached. At this point, the starter unit cuts out automatically.

The start sequence is monitored automatically, and if an engine fails to start, the fuel is cut off, while the engine starter unit continues motoring to ventilate and cool the engine core before another start is attempted. If the second attempt fails to start the engine, the start sequence is aborted. At the end of a successful normal start and with the engines stabilized at idle power, the word 'AVAIL' (available) is displayed on the engine power gauge. On further clearance from the ground engineer, the number-one and number-two engines on the left wing are started simultaneously.

HYDRAULIC SYSTEM

With the four engines running, the eight engine-driven hydraulic pumps, two per engine, are the primary means of pressurizing the 'Green' and 'Yellow' hydraulic systems to a pressure of 5,000psi (345 bar). The 'Green' hydraulic system is supplied by the engines on the left wing, and the 'Yellow' system by those on the right wing. Unlike earlier Airbus aircraft, which have three separate hydraulic systems to allow for redundancy, on the A380, if both the main systems fail, local hydraulic circuits, pressurized by their own small electric pumps, are strategically located at critical flight controls. Thus a complete failure of flying control of the aircraft, owing to total hydraulic loss from both systems, can never occur. Besides the flight controls, the landing gear steering and braking systems are equipped with their own back-up hydraulic circuits. For ground operational needs, when there are no engines running, electrically driven pumps pressurize the 'Green' and 'Yellow' hydraulic systems, allowing the cargo doors to be operated and the aircraft to be towed.

LANDING GEAR

The landing gear consists of a two-wheel nose gear together with a four-bogie, twenty-wheel main gear that supports the maximum 570.0 tonne (561.0imp/628.3US ton) weight of the aircraft. The main gear comprises two six-wheel bogies attached to the belly of the aircraft (the body gear) and two four-wheel bogies located at the wing roots (wing gear). Sixteen of the main landing gear's twenty wheels are equipped with carbon brakes. The nose wheels and the rearmost pair of each body gear bogie do not have any brake units. Brake temperatures and tyre pressures can be monitored on the System Display (SD) by selecting the required wheel schematic on the Electronic Centralized Aircraft Monitoring Control Panel (ECP). Extension and retraction of the landing gear is actuated by both 'Green' and 'Yellow' hydraulic systems, the former controlling the nose and wing gears, and the latter the body gear. In the event of total loss of both hydraulic systems, the landing gear can only be extended by gravity. An electrical signal is used to release the gear uplocks to allow the units to extend under their own weight.

The A380 is steered on the ground by a small handle that operates like a tiller. One of these is situated beside each pilot and is used to turn the nose

The landing gear comprises a two-wheel nose gear, two body gear bogies with six wheels each and two wing gear bogies with four wheels each. (Frikkie Bekker)

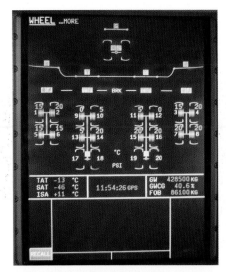

Left: Wheel system display. The wheel temperatures are shown; when 'MORE' is selected, the tyre pressures can also be indicated.

Below left: Landing gear gravity extend switch for emergency extension of the gear following loss of hydraulic power.

Below: Side stick and tiller. The latter is used for making major turns on the ground, while the rudder pedals are employed when slight adjustments of direction are required.

wheel. When making tight turns while taxiing the aircraft in the apron area, however, a set of steerable body gear wheels assists the turning action. Minor changes of direction are achieved by turning the nose wheel with the rudder steering pedals, which give a restricted steering angle. During an automatic landing, limited nose-wheel steering is controlled by the autopilot. The nose-wheel steering is operated primarily by the 'Green' hydraulic system, but in the event of failure, an independent self-contained back-up hydraulic system provides pressure to the steering actuators. During tighter turns, when the nose wheel is rotated to an angle greater than 20 degrees, the body gear steering, powered by the 'Yellow' hydraulic system, is activated. However, only the rearmost pair of wheels on each body bogie are steerable to a maximum of 15 degrees. In spite of its size, therefore, the A380 is capable of making a 180-degree U-turn on a 69m (226ft) wide runway.

Right: Leading-edge, or Kruger, flaps shown in extended position.

Below: Trailing-edge flaps extended for landing.

AFTER START ACTIONS

At the end of the push back, the ground engineer requests that the brakes be set to 'on'. As all four engines are running at this point, the captain proceeds with the after start actions while the ground crew disconnects the push-back tractor. The APU is switched off, the speed brakes are armed and the flaps are run to 'Config 3 Flaps' for the take-off. There are four selectable configurations for the flaps: 1, 2, 3 and Full. For each wing, the flap system comprises six slats and two Kruger flaps on the leading edge, and three sets of slotted flaps on the trailing edge. When the trailing-edge flaps are extended, the ailerons droop downwards to provide extra lift at the extremities of the wings.

Arming the speed brakes signals the stabilizer trim to automatically run to

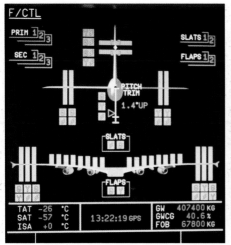

the setting required for take-off for the optimum Take-Off Weight Centre of Gravity (TOWCG) of 39.5 per cent of Mean Aerodynamic Chord (MAC). Unlike previous generations of aircraft, the A380's horizontal stabilizer is adjusted automatically in all flight phases; under normal circumstances, no pilot action is required. Before the taxi is commenced, the side sticks, or joysticks, and rudder pedals are cycled by both pilots and checked for the corresponding correct movement of ailerons, elevators and rudders. As the captain moves the side stick, the Flight Control schematic pops up on the SD, allowing the crew to monitor the control surface movements. Then the captain calls for the After Start checklist, which is selected by the first officer for display on the Engine/Warning Display (EWD). He reads through the list, 'ticking off' the completed items.

TAXI TO THE HOLD

With the after start checks completed, permission to taxi is requested from Heathrow Ground (South). At the busy Heathrow Airport, ATC for taxi, take-off and landing is divided into the North and South control areas. The responsibilities of the airport controllers are further divided into Ground and Tower. After receiving the airways clearance from Heathrow Delivery, the aircraft, being parked at the southern pier six, is transferred to the South Ground movement controller for push-back permission and taxi instructions.

F/O: 'Heathrow Ground, Skybird 380, request taxi.'

Ground: 'Skybird 380, taxi via link thirty-three, Alpha, link twenty-nine, Mike and hold at Lokki.'

ATC at Heathrow Airport has introduced names such as Saturn, Lokki and

Right: Onboard Airport Navigation System (OANS) displayed on the left and taxi video on the right. The flaps and stabilizer settings are depicted below the video.

Far left: Flight Control schematic pops up after engine start to allow movement of the control surfaces to be checked.

Left: After Start checklist displayed on the Engine/ Warning Display (EWD).

Oster for intermediate waiting positions prior to entering the runway holding points. As many aircraft move towards the active runway, these unique names allow easier understanding of instructions. Aircraft wait at these intermediate positions before being directed to the critical holding points at the entries to the runway.

The taxi routing clearance for Runway 27L (left) is read back by the first officer and is shown clearly on the On-Board Airport Navigation System (OANS). The captain releases the brakes and the aircraft starts to roll immediately; even at idle power, the four engines produce sufficient thrust to move the aircraft forward. As a check, the captain eases on the brakes by applying gentle pressure to the pedals, at the same time watching for any pressure change on the brake indicator, located on the forward panel and intended for display of emergency braking only. No movement of the indicator needles shows that brake operation is normal. The aircraft is steered by gentle control of the 'Fly-By-Wire' (FBW) steering handle, turns being taken slowly due to the tendency of the nose wheel to skid, even at low speeds. In a tight turn, 10kt is the maximum recommended speed in dry conditions, while 5kt is the maximum in the wet. As a result, the A380 is taxied a little slower than other airliners.

As the aircraft taxis out, the first officer presses the Rejected Take-Off (RTO) switch to arm the automatic brake system for maximum braking in case the take-off needs to be aborted. Then the 'Take-Off Configuration' test button is pressed on the ECP to ensure that all flaps and the stabilizer trim are in their take-off positions. If any item has been inadvertently omitted, a warning horn sounds to alert the crew that the aircraft is not properly configured for take-off. The captain asks for the before take-off checks. At about this time, the cabin crew member in charge presses a button on the Flight Attendant Panel (FAP) at cabin door M1L to signal that the cabin is ready for departure. This changes the blue 'Cabin Ready' legend to green on

Left: Brake indicator (*top right*) shows that the body gear brake accumulator is pressurized and zero alternate brake pressure is being applied.

Below left: Illuminated 'RTO ARM' button (*bottom left*) indicates that the Rejected Take-Off system is armed for maximum automatic braking in the event of an aborted take-off.

Below: Before Take-Off checklist displayed on the EWD.

the Before Take-Off checklist. The other items on the list are 'ticked off' in turn to ensure that nothing is forgotten. However, the last few items on the checklist are not completed until the final take-off clearance is received from the tower controller.

As the aircraft approaches holding point Lokki, Heathrow Ground (South) hands over control to Heathrow Tower (South). Since the runway in use is 27L (the southern runway), the crew had anticipated the change to the southern tower frequency and had already selected it in the pre-set window of the Radio Management Panel (RMP). At Heathrow, three frequency changes can be expected before a flight becomes airborne, but often at less busy airports, only one radio frequency is used for all the ATC functions of airway clearances, ground movement and tower control.

Ground: 'Skybird 380, monitor Tower, one one eight five.'

To reduce chatter on the busy tower frequency, the crew selects the frequency, but listens only, remaining silent until called.

Tower: 'Skybird 380, taxi to holding point November Two Whiskey.'

F/O: 'Taxi holding point November Two Whiskey, Skybird 380.'

The captain gently increases the power slightly to initiate a quicker taxi to the designated holding point. Ahead, lined up on the runway, is a British Midland A320 aircraft.

Tower: 'British Midland 123, cleared take-off runway two seven left, wind two three zero, ten knots.'

Tower: 'Skybird 380, after departing British Midland three twenty, cleared to line up and hold runway two seven left.'

F/O: 'Cleared to line up and hold runway two seven left after departing, Skybird 380.'

As the other aircraft starts its take-off roll, Skybird 380's captain eases on the power once more to enter the runway, but not before checking to ensure that an aircraft is not on its final landing approach to the runway. Then the captain calls, 'Below the line,' which instructs the first officer to complete the remainder of the before take-off checks. The co-pilot turns on the powerful white flashing strobe lights and landing lights. As a signal to the cabin crew that the aircraft is about to take off, the seat belt signs are cycled to 'off' and then 'on'. The taxi video and OANS are switched back to the PFD and ND respectively, and the weather radars on each side are selected 'on' to display any weather ahead and detect wind shear on the departure track. On take-off, if wind shear is detected, the pilot has the option of stopping if the aircraft speed is below the decision V1 speed or, if above, applying maximum thrust and committing to the take-off.

ENHANCED GROUND PROXIMITY WARNING SYSTEM

If there is high terrain in the vicinity of the airport, the 'Terrain' switch is selected to display that high ground on the first officer's ND. However, this is not an actual image propagated from radar returns, being a computer-generated virtual image of local terrain retrieved from the on-board navigation database of worldwide terrain features. The system is known as the Enhanced Ground Proximity Warning System (EGPWS), and the terrain image superimposed on the ND offers a significant improvement in crew awareness of high ground, especially in poor visibility.

The predecessor to the EGPWS was the Ground Proximity Warning System (GPWS). The latter was introduced in the mid-seventies following the crash of an Eastern Airlines Lockheed Tri-Star in Florida. In that incident, the autopilot was accidentally disconnected when the flight crew became preoccupied with a malfunctioning landing gear indicator light. It was a dark moonless night and the pilots failed to notice that the aircraft was descending gently. With no warning of impending impact, the aircraft continued its descent unnoticed into the Everglades. The accident spurred the introduction of the GPWS. With this system, radio altimeters were used to measure the aircraft's absolute height by bouncing radio signals back from the ground. An excessive height loss or rate of ground closure in the vicinity of terrain triggered the voice warning, 'Terrain! Whoop, whoop! Pull up!' In addition, if the aircraft descended too low without the landing gear or landing flaps extended, owing to an oversight by the crew, the GPWS warning was triggered to alert the pilots to the danger. The EGPWS incorporates the GPWS radio altimeter-based warnings with high-ground awareness warnings from the terrain navigation database. This has added a new dimension to aircraft safety.

CHAPTER 5
TAKE-OFF
AND CLIMB OUT

Tower: 'Skybird 380, cleared for take-off runway two seven left, wind two three zero at ten.'

F/O: 'Cleared for take-off runway two seven left, Skybird 380.'

At the start of the take-off run on the A380, the pilot initially moves the thrust levers manually, as automatic thrust operation is not activated at this stage. The four thrust levers are advanced to 30 per cent power with the aircraft held stationary on the brakes. At this point, the pilots' sense of alertness is heightened. On the A380, thrust power targets are predicated and set as a percentage of the maximum 100 per cent thrust. With the thrust levers at the 30 per cent target, the captain pauses, since the heavy fan blades take fourteen seconds to accelerate and stabilize to the setting. Then, with no abnormal conditions apparent, the captain releases the brakes and manually advances the thrust levers to the 'FLX MCT' (Flexible/Maximum Continuous Thrust) detent. Auto Thrust remains inactive in the 'FLX MCT' detent, but engine power automatically increases to the Flight Management System

On take-off, the thrust levers are placed into the 'FLX MCT' detent, which raises engine power to the thrust level programmed earlier. The red button at the side is the Autothrottle and Autobrake Disconnect button.

(FMS) pre-set take-off flexible thrust of 88 per cent of maximum power. In normal operation, therefore, the A380 thrust levers are more like selector levers than power levers, remaining stationary in the 'FLX MCT' detent as the power increases. If full power is required, the captain can manually advance the thrust levers out of the 'FLX MCT' detent to the furthest forward 'TOGA' (Take Off/Go-Around) detent to demand 100 per cent thrust from the engines.

FLIGHT MODE ANNUNCIATOR

The Flight Mode Annunciator (FMA) indicates the pre-set take-off conditions in the top section of the Primary Flight Display (PFD):

'MAN/FLX' – Manual/Flexible power.
'SRS' – Speed Reference System.
'RWY' – Runway.
'BRK RTO' – Brake Rejected Take-Off.
'CLB' – Climb.
'NAV' – Navigation.
'A/THR' – Auto Thrust.

The FMA is divided into five columns. The first column indicates the commanded thrust mode; the second and third columns show the Flight Director (FD) pitch and roll commands; the fourth column is reserved for approach modes; and the fifth column gives the status of the FDs, autopilots (APs) and Auto Thrust (A/THR) system. Statements in green represent active commands, while those in blue are armed commands awaiting activation on capture. White is used to represent activated modes of the thrust and autopilot systems.

On this particular take-off, 'MAN/FLX' in white in the first column shows that the thrust levers are still in manual mode and that the required detent has to be manually selected for the power to respond accordingly. In the second column, 'SRS' in green indicates that the FD horizontal pitch bar will guide the pilot to hold a speed of V2 plus 10kt during the initial climb. 'RWY' in the third column, also in green, advises that the transmitted localizer signal (giving centreline guidance) of the take-off runway's Instrument Landing System (ILS) has been tuned and that the FD half-length vertical roll bar, shortened to identify its role only for take-off, will provide runway centreline guidance on the take-off run. The FMA also displays 'BRK RTO' in blue, signifying that the RTO mode is armed ready for an emergency stop on the take-off. 'CLB' in blue in the second column means that the climb phase for flap retraction is armed ready for capture. 'NAV', also in blue, in the third column verifies that the navigation system is armed and ready for capture at 50ft, and 'A/ THR' in the last column in blue confirms that the Auto Thrust is armed ready to be activated by the pilot.

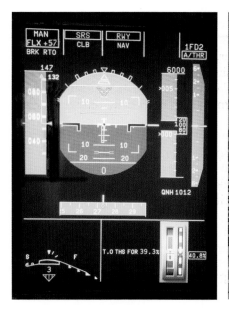
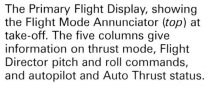

The Primary Flight Display, showing the Flight Mode Annunciator (*top*) at take-off. The five columns give information on thrust mode, Flight Director pitch and roll commands, and autopilot and Auto Thrust status.

The thrust levers are retarded to the 'CL' (Climb) detent at an altitude of 1,500ft to commence the climb phase of the flight following completion of the take-off phase.

AUTO THRUST

At 1,500ft, when take-off power is no longer required, the calculated reduced climb power is set by the captain, who retards the thrust levers from the 'FLX MCT' detent to the 'CL' (Climb) detent. The 'CL' detent also acts as a 'switch' to activate the Auto Thrust; on activation of full Auto Thrust control, the FMA's blue 'A/THR' changes to white to show the active mode. In this instance, therefore, 'Climb detent' is a misnomer, as it should really be called the 'Climb/Auto Thrust' detent.

If an engine fails on take-off, once the flaps have been set to 'up', Maximum Continuous Thrust (MCT), rather than climb thrust, can be selected if required on the remaining three engines. As both the Flex and MCT modes occupy the same detent, to change the setting from Flex to MCT, the pilot manually moves the thrust lever out of, and then back into the 'FLX MCT' detent.

With Auto Thrust in control, the thrust levers remain stationary in the 'CL' detent, untouched by the pilots throughout the climb, cruise, descent, approach and initial landing phase of the flight. Only at the very end of the flight, as the aircraft flares during the landing, does the pilot touch the thrust levers again to manually retard them to idle from the 'CL' detent selection, thereby disconnecting the Auto Thrust system. An automated voice calls out, 'Retard,' at 30ft above the ground as a reminder to the pilot to pull back the levers to the idle detent to disconnect the Auto Thrust mode. At any time in flight, pressing the Auto Thrust disconnect button (there is one on each side of the thrust levers) reverts the levers to full manual control. Then the pilots have to manually move the levers to change the power setting, as on a conventional aircraft.

On take-off, the captain having moved the thrust levers to the 'FLX MCT' detent, the engines roar in response to the take-off power demanded. They are programmed to hesitate at about 70 per cent thrust, however, to reduce excessive fan blade vibrations inherent at ground speeds below 35kt. As 35kt is passed, the thrust increases to the take-off flexible power setting of 88 per cent maximum power.

ENGINES

The A380 on this particular flight is powered by Rolls-Royce Trent 970 engines, each of which is capable of producing a static thrust at sea level in standard conditions of 311kN (70,000lbf). At the time of writing, besides the Trent 900 series, the A380 can be equipped with the Engine Alliance GP7200 engine, a joint venture by the American companies General Electric (GE) and Pratt and Whitney.

The Trent 970 engine is controlled by the Full Authority Digital Engine Control (FADEC), the 'brain' of the power system. Electronic 'Fly-By-Wire' (FBW) signals received by the FADEC from the cockpit thrust levers, or signals from the Auto Thrust control, are used to compute the correct fuel flow to the engines according to the thrust demanded. The FADEC controls the engines in three modes: normal, alternate and degraded. The normal mode is used primarily and is backed up by the alternate mode. If the alternate mode also fails, the lowest level, the degraded mode, takes over. In the alternate and degraded back-up modes, the engines are controlled to targets of N1 (the percentage rotation speed of the fan blades) instead of targets of percentage maximum thrust power. If control of any two engines deteriorates to the degraded mode, the Auto Thrust system becomes unavailable. The FADEC also automatically adjusts and compensates for engine operations when flying through inclement weather such as icing, rain or turbulence. In these conditions, the igniters are automatically turned on and the minimum idle thrust is increased slightly to protect against in-flight engine flame-out. If a flame-out does occur, the FADEC automatically restarts the engine immediately.

During normal operations, engine thrust is extensively managed by the Auto Thrust system, which is used for all aspects of the flight, from the climb phase to the landing. On the captain's movement of the thrust levers to the 'CL' detent at 1,500ft, the Auto Thrust system is activated. Engine thrust retards to the power required for the rest of the climb, as indicated by the

'THR CLB' (Thrust Climb) in column one of the FMA is the desired power setting for the climb phase until the aircraft levels off.

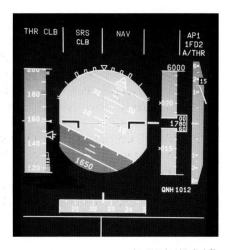

green 'THR CLB' (Thrust Climb) legend on the FMA. If the climb is interrupted by the need to level off at any stage, the Auto Thrust automatically changes from Climb mode to Speed mode to provide sufficient power to maintain the required level flying speed. The other thrust lever detents of '0' (idle power) and 'TOGA' are manually selected to obtain minimum idle power and maximum thrust respectively. If Auto Thrust is already active, placing the levers in either of these two detents deactivates the Auto Thrust system.

THE TAKE-OFF

For the flight in question, a slight cross-wind of 10kt is blowing across the runway from left to right, but is insufficient to lift the left wing. In a stronger wind, however, the pilot would use the side stick to add a small amount of down-aileron on the left wing, reducing its lift slightly. Owing to the sweep-back of the wings, in this case, the left wing is presented at a more direct angle to the wind flow from the left, while the right wing meets it at a more oblique angle. The effect, therefore, is that a sufficiently strong wind from the left would generate more lift from the left wing than the right. Also, in the left–right cross-wind, the aircraft acts like a weather vane, in that the wind bearing on the large tail fin pivots the fuselage on the main landing gear, causing the nose to weathercock to the left. To compensate, the captain depresses the right rudder pedal slightly.

At this stage, the captain's left hand is on the side stick, holding it central, while his right hand is advancing the thrust levers. His feet, with right bias, are on the rudder pedals for steering. Initially, steering is provided by the nose wheel, which keeps the aircraft straight, but as the speed builds, primary directional control is transferred to the rudders as they become effective in the airflow. As the aircraft accelerates, the first officer confirms that the required engine power setting is correctly indicated and announces, 'Thrust set.' The aircraft speed increases, and at the all-important call of 'Eighty knots,' a final cross-check of the airspeed instruments is conducted. If both pilots' instruments are not in agreement, the take-off is immediately aborted. After the 80kt point, the pilot will ignore any minor problems that occur and will only reject the take-off if an engine fails, a flight control problem occurs or the runway is blocked. As the aircraft accelerates past the V1 decision speed of 122kt, a synthesized voice calls out, 'V One.' At this, the captain removes his right hand from the thrust levers and the aircraft is committed to the take-off.

Rejected Take-Off

If a rejected take-off occurs at or close to the V1 speed, the pilot must quickly close the thrust levers and select full reverse power on the two thrust reversers on the numbers two and three (inboard) engines – the outer engines do not have thrust reversers. If one of the thrust reversers is unserviceable, however, the other can still be used on its own. The pilot must confirm the automatic deployment of the speed brakes, or ground spoilers, as this produces aerodynamic drag and, more importantly, forces the weight of the aircraft on to the wheels for more effective braking. On deployment of the ground spoilers, the Rejected Take-Off (RTO) switch that was armed before take-off will trigger the automatic brake to apply full braking with anti-skid protection to stop the aircraft before it reaches the end of the runway. If failures occur after V1, the take-off is continued and any problems are handled once airborne. A high-speed reject is considered a dangerous manoeuvre. Consequently, tyre failures above 100kt are usually ignored and the take-off continued, even if the V1 speed has not been reached.

Lift Off

The next important speed is the rotate speed (VR) of 141kt. When the aircraft reaches this speed, the first officer calls, 'Rotate,' and the captain pulls the side stick gently back to raise the nose at a rate of 3 degrees per second. At that rate, the target of 12.5 degrees nose-up attitude is reached in four seconds. If the nose is lifted too quickly, a tail strike may occur. As the nose passes an attitude of 9 degrees, the weight is taken off the wheels and the aircraft lifts off the ground. At 12.5 degrees nose-up attitude, the captain captures the V2 plus 10kt speed of 156kt for normal climb. If an engine fails at V1, the aircraft can accelerate on the remaining runway and climb at V2 to a minimum height of 35ft above the end of the runway. The V2 speed also ensures the best climb-out angle on three engines to clear any obstacles on the climb path.

Once airborne, the rudders are centred and the captain banks the aircraft slightly left into wind, crabbing the aircraft along the extended runway centreline. At 50ft, the Flight Director (FD) half-length vertical roll bar that was tuned to the runway localizer for centreline guidance on take-off disappears and is replaced by a full-length vertical bar giving lateral guidance. The FMA indication changes from Runway mode to Navigation mode, the

After lift-off, the FMA's third column, representing the roll mode of the Flight Director, changes to 'NAV' at 50ft to guide the pilot on the lateral flight path.

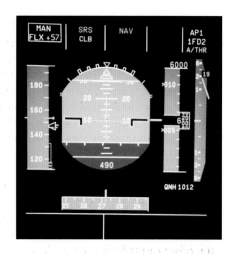

latter's 'NAV' legend flashing green to indicate that the vertical roll bar is following the programmed lateral flight path. The second column displays 'SRS' in green, indicating that the FD horizontal pitch bar has captured the Speed Reference System mode of V2 plus 10kt. At this constant climb speed, the aircraft will ascend at a respectable rate of 2,500ft/min.

The captain calls for gear up, and the first officer operates the gear lever. The landing gear units retract with a thump as they are locked up and the doors close. As the main wheels retract into their bays, they are stopped automatically from spinning by a touch of brake pressure. The nose wheels rub against friction pads as they are stowed in the wheel well. At 100ft, the captain calls 'AP One,' and the first officer selects Autopilot One to 'on' on the Auto Flight System (AFS) control panel. Pilots normally prefer to 'hand fly' the aircraft to an altitude of about 10,000ft before switching to the autopilot, but as Heathrow is a noise-sensitive airport, any deviation from the required Standard Instrument Departure (SID) track could infringe noise-restricted areas. Monitoring units situated close to the SID tracks measure noise levels to ensure accurate flying of the take-off route so that the least disturbance is caused to the neighbourhood. If an aircraft's noise level exceeds the limit or, as pilots say, 'rings the bell', a hefty fine is levied on the airline. Since the autopilot can follow a more accurate track than the pilot, it is selected to fly the aircraft as early as possible.

FLIGHT CONTROLS

When the pilot is manually flying the aircraft, the side stick and rudder pedal inputs are fed to six flight control computers, which determine the movement of the flight control surfaces. Unlike the Boeing 747 and other earlier commercial aircraft, where pilot inputs are directly linked by conventional cables and pulleys to units that operate the control surfaces, the A380 utilizes a control concept that is fully FBW. Signals from the pilot's inputs are transmitted by flight control computers along electrical wires to operate the flying controls without any mechanical connection. Any pilot input, however, is verified by the computers before being transmitted to the controls; only logical commands can be accepted to operate the control surfaces. Extreme manoeuvres by the pilot that may over-control the aircraft or induce a stall are not accepted. It could be said, therefore, that the pilot is never in direct control of the flight control surfaces.

The primary flight controls consist of two pairs of elevators, two rudder surfaces and three pairs of ailerons. The ailerons also function as droop flaps for take-off, and as spoilers for landing to augment the effects of the flap and spoiler systems. There are slats and Kruger flaps at the wing leading edges, inboard, mid- and outboard flaps at the trailing edges, and four pairs of spoilers on the top of each wing. The horizontal stabilizer, or movable tailplane, controls the aircraft's trim automatically in all phases of flight, even when the aircraft is flown manually, and is hydraulically operated with a manual electrically controlled back-up facility. The rudders can also be manually trimmed, but are automatically trimmed when the autopilot has been selected. There is no aileron trim on the A380.

The primary 'muscle' power for operating most of the flying control surfaces is provided by the 'Green' and 'Yellow' hydraulic systems. Some control surfaces are equipped with their own separate, self-contained, electric powered hydraulic systems and are known as Electrostatic Hydraulic Actuators (EHAs). Within the actuator package, they have their own hydraulic circuit and electric pump. A second type of back-up for the control surfaces is the Electrical Back-Up Hydraulic Actuator (EBHA), which functions as both a conventional and an electrostatic hydraulic actuator. If the EBHA's main hydraulic supply fails, an electrically powered hydraulic circuit is activated to provide the power to drive the actuators for control movement.

Any one of the six computers, three 'prims' (primary) and three 'secs' (secondary), controlling the flying control surfaces is capable of totally managing all the flying controls, including modulating and compensating all stick and rudder inputs. The side-stick control for each pilot, unlike the conventional control yoke on other aircraft, operates independently and in isolation; to the disappointment of most pilots, it provides no tactile feedback to the other pilot. Movement of the side stick on one side, therefore, does not move the other pilot's side stick, which remains in its neutral position. If both pilots use their respective side sticks simultaneously, the sum of both the commands is sent to the computers. For example, if both pilots were to pull their side sticks half-way back, the resultant sum of full aft stick would be passed to the computers. Since this particular situation would be undesirable, it is procedurally prohibited. If one pilot wishes to take control from the other, a side stick take-over button must be pressed to disable the other pilot's stick. The pilot pressing the take-over button will have full control of the aircraft. The rudder pedals, however, are closed loop – movement on one side is mirrored by movement on the other.

When pushed, a small red button on the top of the side stick allows the pilot to disable the other stick and assume full control of the aircraft. The same button is used to disconnect the autopilot.

The FBW system makes flying the A380 much easier and more stable, pilot commands being computed into a flight trajectory command. The flight computers compensate for external forces, such as wind gusts or even the yawing effect of an engine failure, that tend to upset the aircraft's flight path. During all phases of flight except landing, the process by which the computers govern the flight controls is under the authority of three 'laws': Normal, Alternate and Direct. When the primary computers are in full control of the aircraft, the flight controls are deemed to be in Normal Law and are protected against exceeding the maximum bank angle, pitch attitude and angle of attack. Normal Law also prevents flight at excessive or insufficient speed, and overstress and/or overload of the aircraft wing structures. The protection against excessive angles of attack, for example, stops the aircraft from approaching a stall condition. When landing, Normal Law changes to Flare Law below 100ft, whereupon there is a direct relationship between the pilot's inputs and the movement of the control surfaces, just as on a conventional aircraft. At the landing stage, therefore, the pilot has full control of the elevators to allow accurate judgement of when to flare the aircraft during the touchdown.

If several minor failures occur at the same time, the Normal Law flight control process degrades to Alternate Law and some flight protection is lost. Instead of high- and low-speed protection, Alternate Law provides high- and low-speed stability, which results in the aircraft pitching up or down as necessary when its limiting speeds are approached. It pitches up for an over-speed situation and down when the speed drops too low. There is no bank angle or pitch attitude protection in Alternate Law. If all three primary flight computers fail, leaving the secondary computers to take over, the control process reverts to Direct Law, the lowest computed status. Under Direct Law, the controls function very much like those of a conventional aircraft, with neither flight protection nor stabilizer auto trim available, the pilot being required to manually trim the aircraft with two trim switches located on the lower centre console.

In the very unlikely event of a total failure of all six flight computers, an electrical back-up mode is available, which directs unmodified pilot control inputs to certain flight control actuators. In this mode, only one aileron on each wing, two elevators and two rudders are active to provide a temporary – and sluggish – emergency control that allows time for the pilots to attempt to rectify the computer fault and recover full control. In the electrical back-up mode, operation of the flight controls is not meant to provide the ability to carry out a safe landing.

CLIMB OUT

As Skybird 380 proceeds on the published SID, the autopilot turns the aircraft positively to the left to track to the Epsom Non-Directional Beacon (NDB). The SIDs at Heathrow are still predicated on tracking from beacon to beacon, so the captain selects the NDB on the Electronic Flight Instrument System (EFIS) panel to display the NDB positions on the Navigation Display (ND). As expected, the aircraft is tracking precisely towards the Epsom beacon, verifying the accurate flying of the autopilot under the guidance of the Inertial Reference System (IRS) navigation.

Skybird 380 climbs quickly with take-off power set and, at 1,500ft above the airport, thrust is reduced by the captain moving the thrust levers to the 'CL' detent. If this detent selection is overlooked, 'LVR CLB' (Lever Climb) flashes on the FMA to remind the pilot to reposition the lever. With levers in the 'CL' detent, the Auto Thrust system activates and sets the commanded climb thrust, maintaining the engine climb power program until the aircraft levels off at the top of the climb. On the FMA, the first column representing the engine Auto Thrust target changes from 'MAN FLX' to 'THR CLB'. In the second FMA column, the FD horizontal bar remains in SRS mode and holds the captured V2 plus 10kt speed to the programmed altitude of 4,000ft, where flap retraction begins. On passing 4,000ft, the SRS mode on the FMA will change to the CLB mode, which will accelerate the aircraft to allow flap

The NDB selector button on the Electronic Flight Instrument System (EFIS) panel lights up when pressed and displays the NDB data on the Navigation Display.

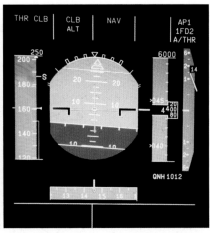

'LVR CLB' (Lever Climb), displayed in the first column of the FMA, flashes on passing 1,500ft to remind the pilot to retard the thrust lever to the 'CL' detent for the climb phase.

The second column (Flight Director pitch guidance) changes from 'SRS' (Speed Reference System) to 'CLB' (Climb) as the aircraft accelerates for flaps retraction.

retraction and then hold 250kt climb speed until the aircraft passes 10,000ft (flight level 100). Above that level, the CLB mode will hold the most efficient climb speed of about 330kt until reaching cruise level, barring any ATC restrictions.

At 4,000ft, the nose lowers and the aircraft accelerates from the V2 plus 10kt initial climb speed to the first flap retraction speed. The 'Config 3 Flaps' take-off setting is maintained until the aircraft accelerates past a green letter 'F' on the speed tape on the PFD. Then the flaps are selected directly to 'Config 1 Flaps'. The 'Config 2 Flaps' setting is bypassed because the acceleration of the aircraft quickly puts it in the 'Config 1 Flaps' domain, leaving no time to select the intermediate setting. However, 'Config 2 Flaps' is used on the approach to land.

At the captain's call of 'Flaps one,' the co-pilot operates the flap lever, and the trailing edge flap is seen to run on the flap indicator, located on the lower part of the PFD, from the 'Flaps 3' position to 'Flaps 1+F'. The next flap retraction speed is about 50kt above Vref (the minimum flyable reference speed with full flap set at the present aircraft weight) and is marked by a green letter 'S' on the PFD speed tape. At the appropriate speed, the captain calls, 'Flaps zero,' and the flaps are selected up. The first officer watches the flap indicator and, on seeing the flaps fully retracted, calls, 'Flaps are zero.' Then the captain requests the after take-off checks; the checklist is selected and displayed by the first officer on the EWD, being completed silently.

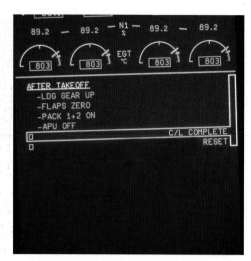

Left: After the flaps have been retracted, the After Take-Off checklist is selected and completed by the Pilot Not Flying (PNF).

Right: Altitude constraint of 6,000ft is deleted following clearance from ATC.

Far right: Standard (STD) pressure setting is selected by pressing the altimeter button on the left of the EFIS control panel.

Tower: 'Skybird 380, call Control, one two zero five two.'

F/O: 'One two zero five two, Skybird 380.'

The first officer switches to the pre-selected London Control frequency and makes the radio call.

F/O: 'Afternoon Control, Skybird 380 Super, passing two thousand feet on the Detling two golf departure.'

The suffix 'Super' is added on initial contact with terminal controllers, in line with the International Civil Aviation Organization (ICAO) rules, to indicate that the aircraft is an A380 and that a greater separation from other aircraft is required to prevent them from encountering its wake turbulence.

Control: 'Skybird 380, squawk ident.'

The first officer selects 'Ident' (identification) on the Radio Management Panel (RMP) and presses the transponder 'Ident' button. In the air traffic centre, the radar controller sees a flashing flight number on the radar screen that confirms the communicating aircraft's identity.

Control: 'Skybird 380, identified, climb flight level one four zero, unrestricted.'

The first officer reads back the clearance and, as the flight is cleared to bypass the first SID altitude constraint of 6,000ft, the captain enters the new altitude of 14,000ft (flight level 140) in the altitude window on the AFS panel. The SID restricted altitude of 6,000ft is still programmed in the FMS, however,

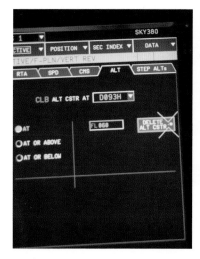

and the limit must be removed. If not, the aircraft will level off at 6,000ft instead of climbing to the cleared level of FL140. The first officer calls up the Constraints page on the Multi-Function Display (MFD) and, with a click, removes the altitude restriction, allowing the autopilot to proceed on a continuous climb to FL140.

As the aircraft climbs through 6,000ft, the transition altitude, the pilots press the altimeter pressure-setting knobs on their EFIS panels to change the Heathrow area pressure setting of 1012hP (hectoPascals – formerly millibars) to the 'standard' pressure setting of 1013hP. Since all aircraft above the transition altitude are required to have their altimeters adjusted to this standard pressure setting, accurate vertical separation is maintained as they cruise at their allocated levels along the airways. Aircraft heights below the transition altitude are referred to as altitudes, and above as flight levels. Thus Skybird 380's cleared height of 14,000ft, set to standard pressure, is referred to as flight level one four zero.

THE AUTOPILOTS

As the captain is the Pilot Flying (PF), Autopilot One (AP1) is selected to fly the aircraft for all phases of the flight; Autopilot Two (AP2) is used if the first officer is designated PF. Only one of the A380's two autopilots is employed at a time, except in the critical phase of an Auto Land, when both are selected, one being in control and the other in standby mode. The autopilots receive their directions from the FMS, which is programmed by the pilots during the pre-flight preparations to provide the autopilot with the parameters of the required lateral and vertical flight profiles. If programmed properly, in theory, the A380 autopilot and Auto Thrust system can fly the route all the way from selection at 100ft after take-off to an automatic landing and complete stop on the runway at the aircraft's destination with very little intervention from the

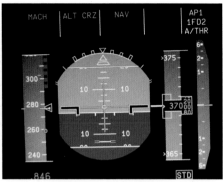

Above: The FMA shows that Autopilot One ('AP1') with Auto Thrust ('A/THR') is flying a constant Mach speed at the aircraft's cruise altitude ('ALT CRZ') along the planned route ('NAV').

Left: Changes to the Flight Management System (FMS) programming can be made via the Keyboard and Cursor Control Unit (KCCU).

pilot, assuming, of course, that there are no ATC or weather impediments along the way. Such a scenario is unrealistic, however, since many changes and adjustments can be expected on a flight.

The FMS program can be adjusted via the MFD using the Keyboard and Cursor Control Units (KCCUs), or the cursor with track and ball. When the FMS is in control of the autopilot, it is said to be in the Managed mode; when the pilot controls the autopilot by making selections on the AFS control panel, it is termed to be in the Selected mode. Pilot control of the autopilot is easily achieved with the AFS knobs – the pilot simply pulls the knobs for the Selected mode to take control of the autopilot, and simply pushes the knobs back in to return automatic control to the FMS computer.

All autopilot changes are displayed on the FMA in green to show that they are in the captured active mode, or in blue if they are in the armed mode. The pilots must call the changes as they appear on the FMA display to verify that the autopilot is performing the correct actions and to keep both pilots 'in the loop' in the operation of the aircraft. With the current high degree of automation, the challenge for today's aircraft designers is to minimize problems and misunderstandings at the interface between human and machine. As more automation is introduced into the cockpit, manufacturers are faced with finding new ways to keep the human pilots informed of what is going on; many aural and visual prompts are used to alert the crew to the changes that occur within the aircraft's automatic systems. With advances in technology, the human/machine interface has been greatly improved, but pilots must still remain vigilant, exercise caution and be sceptical of the automatic systems at all times.

The use of the autopilot enhances safety, as it prevents operation outside the aircraft's safe flight envelope, something that can occur under human control. More importantly, automation reduces the workload of the pilots, which improves situational awareness and safety. In fact, in foggy conditions, it is normal procedure for the pilots to allow the automatic systems to land the aircraft. In Auto Land, the autopilot captures and follows the airport's Instrument Landing System (ILS) down to a landing, bringing the aircraft to a complete stop on the runway. The ILS emits radio transmissions for the aircraft to follow from two antennas on the ground. One is at the side of the runway and transmits glide slope (descent path) guidance; the other is at the far end and transmits localizer (centreline) guidance. Automatic landing capability on the ILS is classified at three levels of accuracy, namely Category 1, 2 or 3, with Category 3 being subdivided into Category 3A, 3B and 3C, depending on the quality and accuracy of the ILS transmissions, and the aircraft's avionics systems. In Category 3C conditions, the aircraft can virtually land 'blind' in zero visibility.

Due to the navigational accuracy guaranteed by Global Positioning System (GPS) updating, at airports that do not have an ILS, the A380 can follow a self-produced pseudo ILS profile, called the FMS Landing System (FLS), on the approach to the runway. The FMS database stores a pre-programmed FLS for all airports. At the time of writing, however, FMS guidance can only be used in less exacting circumstances than Category 3 down to short final, where the runway is sighted and a visual landing is made.

TEAMWORK

Skybird 380 continues the climb at a restricted speed of 250kt, the maximum speed allowed by ATC in the terminal area, until passing FL100. Then it accelerates to an efficient climb speed of 327kt. As the altimeter climbs past 10,000ft, both pilots call, 'Flight level one hundred,' which is a standard call procedure practised by crews to increase awareness and enhance teamwork. Such practices are enshrined in company Standard Operating Procedures (SOPs), which ensure commonality of flight operations in all normal and abnormal situations. All crew members are trained to operate an aircraft type in a certain way, with little variation, and to use standardized terms that are easy to understand. Once a year, airline crews are subjected to a 'line check', their performance being observed on a normal revenue flight to ensure adherence to company procedures and that no personal habits or styles are introduced into the operations. During a line check, the pilots' aircraft flight management and inter-personal skills are also rated.

In modern airline operations, teamwork is essential for safety. At great cost, airlines support Cockpit Resource Management (CRM) training and invest a great deal in human performance courses. Individualistic 'ace pilot' tendencies are totally unacceptable, and consultation between crew members, with opinions being shared, is positively encouraged. In the seventies, it became apparent that pilot error was the main cause of accidents and that too much authority was being vested in one crew member, namely the captain. With pilots being susceptible to error, it was recognized that a more consultative approach, where all crew members participated in the decision-making process, enhanced safety. In today's operational environment, it is normal for cockpit crew to cross-check each other, and for subordinate crew members to voice opinions and, in extreme cases, even to take over the aircraft from the captain.

CREW ACTIONS IN THE CLIMB

Climbing past FL100 is the cue for the crew to turn off the landing lights, which are used below that level as a 'see and be seen' precaution. The seat belt signs are also turned off, conditions permitting. The second Very High Frequency (VHF) radio, which is not normally used for ATC communication, is tuned to the international distress frequency of 121.5MHz (megahertz) for monitoring. All commercial flights maintain a listening watch on this frequency at all times, pilots using it occasionally to raise another aircraft so that they can both switch to a 'chat' frequency, such as 123.45MHz, to pass messages.

The seat belt sign being turned off is also the signal for the cabin crew to begin their in-flight service duties. The entertainment system is switched on, and the cabin temperature and lights are adjusted using touch-screen controls on the Flight Attendant Panel (FAP), which is located in the cabin forward of door M1L. The cabin crew also starts heating the pre-cooked meals for lunch.

Left: The Flight Attendant Panel (FAP) alongside main door one left (M1L) is used to select the cabin environment settings.

Right: With the weather radar indicating cloud ahead, the aircraft is turned to a heading of 120 degrees, away from the planned route.

Far right: When clear of the weather, 'DIRECT TO KOK' is selected from the list of forward waypoints on the Multi-Function Display (MFD).

WEATHER DIVERSION

From Skybird 380's flight deck, the crew can see a large threatening cloud formation looming about 40nm ahead, and a request for a 10nm deviation to the right of track to avoid the weather is granted. The captain pulls the heading knob to steer a heading of 120 degrees and the aircraft turns away from the build-up. Ten minutes later, with the weather on the left, a direct track to position Koksy (KOK) is requested. London approves the request and the first officer selects the 'DIR' (direct) button on the KCCU. A list of waypoints ahead is displayed on the MFD. Waypoint KOK is selected and 'direct to' executed, and the aircraft tracks directly to Koksy.

FLIGHT TIMES

During the climb, the first officer begins to deal with the necessary paperwork, including filling in the paper flight log by adding the times to all the programmed waypoints. If the en-route winds and temperatures at high altitude had not been entered into the FMS during the pre-flight preparations, at this point the co-pilot would send a datalink request for the data so that the FMS could be updated. With the winds and temperatures entered, an accurate estimate of the times for all the waypoints and the destination can be provided, as well as the Estimated Fuel On Board (EFOB) for each waypoint. The data also update the times on the flight progress display on the in-flight entertainment screen at each passenger's seat.

MACH NUMBER

As Skybird 380 continues to climb, London Control hands over to another London radar sector, and the aircraft is re-cleared to its cruise level of FL370.

As the altimeters wind past FL200, the pilots call out 'Two hundred,' and at FL300, the standard call of 'Three hundred,' is given. At these higher levels, the speed target on the PFD transitions from an indicated air speed (IAS) to a Mach number. The autopilot adjusts the nose-up attitude to hold a climb speed of Mach 0.84, representing 84 per cent of the speed of sound in the ambient conditions. As the altitude increases, the ambient temperature falls and, since the speed of sound is dependent on temperature, climbing at the constant Mach number of 0.84 results in a decrease in ground speed.

ATTAINING CRUISE LEVEL

Passing FL360, the pilots make the standard call of 'One thousand to go,' meaning 1,000ft to the target level. As the cruise level of FL370 is reached, the FMA changes in the autopilot vertical mode from 'CLB' to 'ALT CRZ' (Cruise Altitude). The Auto Thrust transits from the climb power setting to a speed-holding mode to maintain the most efficient cruise speed for the A380 of about Mach 0.84. The FMA thrust indication changes from 'THR CLB' to 'MACH' (Cruise Speed). In this mode, thrust is automatically modulated to maintain the cruise speed as commanded by the FMS.

CHAPTER 6
THE CRUISE

In the cruise, the Auto Thrust system downgrades to a 'softer' mode to improve passenger comfort and does not react too quickly to slight changes in speed. The efficient Mach speed of around 0.84 maintained at this altitude translates to a true airspeed of 479kt. Since Skybird 380 enjoys the benefit of a 15kt tail-wind, a ground speed of 494kt is indicated on the Navigation Display (ND).

Ideally an aircraft should be flown between its optimum and maximum cruise altitudes for the most efficient fuel consumption. At the optimum cruise level, fuel efficiency is greatest; at the maximum cruise level, the rarefied air results in the aircraft flying close to the stall at the lower end of the speed range and near the maximum Mach speed at the higher end. Pilots refer to this predicament as 'coffin corner' and avoid flying at such levels, where flight safety can be compromised if turbulence from a jet stream or high cloud forces the aircraft beyond the narrow safe speed margins.

In general, as fuel is burned and weight reduces, the aircraft climbs in steps to maintain cruise altitudes between the optimum and maximum flight levels. At Skybird 380's weight, 10 tonnes (9.8imp/11.0US tons) of fuel is burned between take-off and the top of the climb; with 12 tonnes (11.8imp/13.2US tons) of fuel being burned per hour at cruise level with all four engines running, the aircraft will step climb 2,000ft every three hours.

The Cruise Performance page of the Flight Management System (FMS) shows an optimum cruise altitude ('OPT') of flight level 370 and a maximum capable cruise altitude ('REC MAX') of flight level 395.

A video camera allows the pilots to monitor the area between the cockpit security door and the access door from the main cabin.

COCKPIT ENTRY

At the top of the climb, a cabin crew member serves refreshments to the pilots. Before gaining access to the cockpit, however, the crew member has to call on the interphone to obtain permission. Then a code number is entered to release the lock and allow passage through the first of two cockpit doors. After closing the door, the cabin crew member presses a chime button on the second door to alert the pilot to unlock it. Before doing so, the pilot checks the area between the doors on a video monitor to verify the identity of the visitor. The second cockpit entrance door is a bulletproof security door capable of withstanding attacks from high-velocity assault rifles. Since it is just about lunchtime, the cabin crew member also takes the pilots' meal orders. As a precaution against food poisoning, the captain and co-pilot always choose different meals.

CONTROLLER PILOT DATA LINK COMMUNICATION

Since the London/Maastricht air traffic control boundary is approaching, the first officer selects the Air Traffic Control (ATC) communication page on the Multi-Function Display (MFD) and enters the four-letter code 'EDYY' to establish datalink communications with the Brussels ATC Upper Information Region (UIR). The datalink allows typed messages to pass between pilot and controller via a system called Controller Pilot Data Link Communication (CPDLC), instead of employing Very High Frequency (VHF) radio voice transmissions, thus freeing the airwaves from chatter, which is especially useful during times of heavy air traffic. The message 'ACTIVE ATC: EDYY' flashes on the bottom portion of the System Display (SD), aptly called the ATC Mailbox, to indicate that the system is ready for use.

CPDLC is part of the Future Air Navigation System (FANS), which was

At the bottom of the System Display (SD) is the ATC Mailbox, which shows messages sent via the Controller Pilot Data Link Communication (CPDLC) system. This message states that Maastricht ATC is in active control.

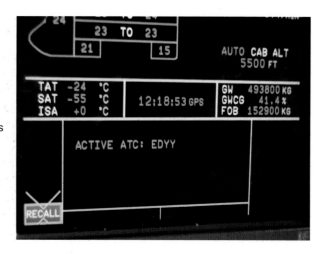

introduced in the early nineties. In 1983, the International Civil Aviation Organization (ICAO) formed a study group to look at a fresh concept of air traffic management that relied on new ways of communicating, navigating and monitoring air traffic that would revolutionize the task. At that time, the Aircraft Communications Addressing and Reporting System (ACARS) was in operation, using satellite and VHF radio communications networks. Rather than wait for the development of a more advanced communications system, ICAO decided to launch FANS-A with an ACARS datalink network. ACARS, initially used for information and company communications, was upgraded with on-board Air Traffic Service Units (ATSUs) that permitted the establishment of the CPDLC function, thus allowing communication by printed word between the pilot and ground controller. Although the 'free texting' of messages was possible, just like texting on mobile phones, most communication between pilots and controllers was by the use of pre-set standard phrases. The pilot simply chose the required message from a list and sent a request, reply or an acknowledgement of compliance to an instruction. If required, all CPDLC messages can be printed as hardcopies by the on-board printer.

In the early nineties, the CPDLC system was tested in the remote South Pacific. During these initial trials, it proved a welcome relief to flight crews who previously had endured difficulties caused by static noise and radio interference when transmitting long-range position reports by High Frequency (HF) radio. By contrast, CPDLC datalink messages do not suffer from interference, or from miscommunication and ambiguity, as the messages are in printed format and, unlike voice communications, cannot be misheard. Progressively, CPDLC spread from remote areas to regions with busy airways, such as Europe. The system has proved unpopular with pilots in Europe, however, owing to the time lag between messages and the inconvenience of typing them out. As a result, communication with ATC by VHF radio voice transmissions is preferred.

NEW NAVIGATION SYSTEMS

In an effort to improve navigation, FANS introduced the concepts of Area Navigation (RNAV), Required Navigation Performance (RNP) and Reduced Vertical Separation Minimum (RVSM). On the A380, a hybrid of three Inertial Reference Systems (IRS) and two Global Positioning Systems (GPS) provides navigation accuracy and ensures integrity of the aircraft position in the Flight Management System (FMS). The FMS is performance monitored and the navigational accuracy updated by GPS or, when within range, by en-route Distance Measuring Equipment (DME) radios, which are automatically tuned by the FMS computer. The system provides highly accurate navigation in all regions, independent of ground-based navigation equipment. An on-board alerting system warns of degraded performance, while the pilot can check its accuracy at any time by selecting the 'Monitor' button on the MFD. On the basis of this highly accurate on-board equipment, RNAV was introduced.

RNAV airways for properly equipped aircraft are characteristically drawn as straight lines on maps, as opposed to the zigzagging tracks of conventional airways. Direct, long-distance great-circle routes with reduced longitudinal and lateral separation between aircraft are also allowed, providing greater use of available airspace. Within RNAV-defined airspace, the concept of 'free flight' will be permitted, whereby aircraft can fly on any desired flight path. Airlines will be able to plan direct routings between departure and destination airports, free of published airways and tracks, thereby saving substantial amounts of fuel.

In RNAV areas, the accuracy and dependability of navigation systems must be assured, and the on-board equipment must comply with what is termed the Required Navigation Performance. For RNP operations in RNAV-defined airspace, the equipment must be able to demonstrate that any

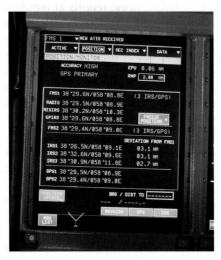

The navigational accuracy of the aircraft is displayed on the Monitor page. In this case, the accuracy is 'HIGH' (to within 0.06nm).

navigation error will not exceed the specified RNP nautical mile limit for 95 per cent of the time on any given flight. As an example, the limit for an RNAV Pacific Ocean crossing is RNP 10, which means that the aircraft must be accurately navigated to within 10nm of track for 95 per cent of the flight. The RNP on RNAV routes is dictated by the air traffic authorities and typically ranges from 4 to 12nm, with better RNP performances being required to allow closer separation between aircraft. RNP 4, for example, allows longitudinal and lateral separation between aircraft of 30nm, while RNP 10 provides a 50nm separation. RNAV routes over oceanic and remote areas require RNP 10, and over continental areas RNP 5. In airport terminal areas, RNAV Standard Instrument Departures (SIDs), Standard Terminal Arrival Routes (STARs) and approaches to land require RNP 0.3 to 1.

At the time of writing, ICAO is moving towards the concept of Performance Based Navigation (PBN) as a common standard for worldwide navigation specifications. PBN goes beyond the accuracy concept of RNP, encompassing performance requirements for accuracy, integrity, continuity and availability, as well as specifying how these requirements are to be achieved by aircraft and crew.

Another aspect of FANS is the Reduced Vertical Separation Minimum. RVSM halved the vertical separation between aircraft on opposite-direction airways above flight level 290 from 2,000ft to 1,000ft and doubled the traffic density of the airspace. Improved on-board altimetry equipment and revised crew monitoring procedures were mandated to ensure very accurate vertical separation between aircraft.

Air Traffic Management (ATM) surveillance in FANS is by conventional secondary radar in local areas, and by Automatic Dependent Surveillance (ADS), a satellite-based position monitoring system, in more remote regions. ATM surveillance allows controllers to monitor the progress of flights worldwide without any direct voice communication with the pilots. Once again, ACARS is used to transmit aircraft FMS position reports at required points along the airway to ATC centres; controllers can also request position data from the aircraft at any time. Real-time ADS monitoring obviates the need for traditional voice position reports by radio, as the aircraft transmits its position automatically at five-minute intervals.

FANS, of late known technically as Communication Navigation Surveillance/Air Traffic Management (CTN/ATM), is being improved from the initial FANS-A towards the targeted FANS-B level. FANS operations began with the CPDLC via ACARS, but that is being superseded by a new communications network, the Aeronautical Telecommunication Network (ATN). Automatic Dependent Surveillance-Broadcast (ADS-B) is also being introduced to provide ground controllers with improved real-time monitoring of aircraft and to allow suitably equipped aircraft to monitor each other in the same airspace. With ADS-B, aircraft traffic in the vicinity can be depicted on the aircraft's Navigation Display (ND), very much like the present Traffic Alert and Collision Avoidance System (TCAS). The system is

The top of the pilot's pull-out table unfolds to reveal a keyboard. This is used to operate the On-Board Information Terminal (OIT) and should not be confused with the Keyboard and Cursor Control Unit (KCCU) below the Multi-Function Display (MFD), which is used for FMS work and ATC communications.

called Air Traffic Situation Awareness (ATSAW). In addition, it contributes to the concept of 'free flight', whereby aircraft will be able to monitor and maintain their own separation.

On the A380, FANS datalink messages are passed via Satcom (satellite communication), HF radio, VHF transmissions through VHF Omni-Range (VOR) radio beacons and Mode S transponders, being managed by the pilots on the ATC sub-section of the MFD. For ATC monitoring, the FMS interfaces with the ATSUs to provide information for ADS and position reporting. To send messages via the CPDLC, the crew uses the MFD and the Keyboard Cursor Control Unit (KCCU) to type messages into the ATC Mailbox on the lower portion of the SD, before dispatching them to the relevant ATC centres. Deviations for weather, route changes and changes in flight levels are requested in this manner. Replies and other messages sent from ground stations via CPDLC are also displayed in the ATC Mailbox, and hard copies can be created using the on-board printer. In addition, the Airline Operational Control (AOC) section of ACARS is used for passing information to and from the company's operations centre. This is displayed on the On-Board Information Terminal (OIT). The AOC is also connected to the aircraft warning computers, malfunction messages being sent automatically to base. The crew can send messages via the AOC by typing them on the keyboard located beneath the hinged top of each pilot's fold-away table.

DATALINK MESSAGING

As the aircraft approaches the Koksy waypoint, London Control hands over the flight to Maastricht ATC.

London Control: 'Skybird 380, contact Maastricht Control, one three two seven five. Good-day.'

F/O: 'Maastricht, one three two seven five. Good-day.'

F/O: 'Good afternoon Maastricht Control, Skybird 380 maintaining flight level three seven zero. Datalink established.'

The phrase 'Datalink established', informs the controller that two-way communication is available via CPDLC.

Maastricht Control: 'Good afternoon Skybird 380. Roger, identified.'

A moment later, a sound like a telephone ringing is heard in the cockpit, and a blue flashing button labelled 'ATC MSG' (ATC message) illuminates on the glare shield. The pilot presses the flashing button to reset it and checks the message in the ATC Mailbox. The datalink message 'Cleared present position direct Bombi' is displayed. To acknowledge the instructions, the pilot selects 'Roger' (message received), which is a pre-set message on the screen, and presses 'Send'. As standard procedure, the pilot also reads back the instruction over the VHF radio frequency.

F/O: 'Skybird 380, datalink, present position direct Bombi.'

Maastricht Control: 'Roger, Skybird 380.'

AIRCRAFT SEPARATION

Aircraft under radar control can expect to be given many 'short-cuts' to bypass intermediate waypoints, and on this occasion Maastricht Control has cleared the flight direct from its present position to Bombi, a waypoint near the city of Frankfurt. Using the cursor control to select the command 'Direct to' on the MFD turns the aircraft towards Bombi.

A light on the front glare shield illuminates to attract the pilots' attention when an ATC message is received.

The frequency for the next ATC control region, Rhine, is checked on the Jeppesen en-route chart and pre-selected on the Radio Management Panel (RMP). Reduced Vertical Separation Minimum (RVSM) has been implemented for some time over Europe, and over much of the globe, and as Skybird 380 is heading in an easterly direction, it occupies only odd flight levels – such as 290, 310, 330, 350, 370, 390 and 410 – with reciprocal traffic flying at even flight levels – 300, 320, 340, 360, 380 and 400.

With the paperwork out of the way, and having double-checked the pre-programmed routing to the destination, the crew settles down to the routine task of monitoring the navigation and maintaining communications with ATC. The captain picks up the handset located on the centre console and makes a public address (PA) to the passengers, informing them of the flight's progress and the all-important Expected Time of Arrival (ETA) at Dubai. The boom microphone of the pilot's headset can be employed for such announcements, but it is rarely used. The reason is that pilots have been known to select the incorrect transmit button when using the boom mike, leading to PA announcements being broadcast over the airwaves rather than into the cabin. The transmissions jam the control radio frequency and, when the announcement ends, invite many a ribald remark from pilots of other aircraft on the same frequency.

Over Europe, where there is full radar coverage, no position reports are necessary, ATC radar maintaining a separation of at least 5nm between aircraft flying in the same direction and at the same level. In more remote regions, where no radar monitoring of aircraft progress is available, pilots must transmit position reports to ATC units, giving the time of crossing each waypoint, the aircraft's flight level and the estimated time at the next waypoint. Using these position reports, the controller ensures horizontal separation between aircraft based on a time span of 10–15 minutes, depending on local ATC requirements. On most oceanic crossings, aircraft are spaced at fifteen-minute intervals. This can be reduced to ten minutes, however, when one aircraft is following another at the same level and both can maintain the same controlled speed.

After a short while, the cabin crew member returns with the meals, which the pilots eat from proper pull-out tables in front of them, unlike on other aircraft types where meals are eaten from trays on laps. The pull-out table concept is unique to Airbus aircraft and is immensely popular with pilots.

FLIGHT INFORMATION REGIONS

As Skybird 380 proceeds towards the German Flight Information Region (FIR), another datalink message is received. The crew is instructed to change to the Rhine Control radio frequency, and the first officer sends an acknowledgement. The FIR is the limit of the local air traffic authority's area of jurisdiction. FIRs usually follow a country's political boundaries, although sometimes for practical purposes they extend into neighbouring countries'

Each pilot is provided with a pull-out table (visible on the right), which acts as a worktop and also provides a surface for taking meals.

airspace. A typical example would be the Singapore FIR, where the area of control intrudes over Malaysian territory to the north and Indonesian territory to the south.

A datalink message from Maastricht Control, 'FROM EDYY CTL NEXT ATC EDUU', appears in the ATC Mailbox, indicating that transfer of the CPDLC to Rhine Centre is imminent. As Skybird 380 enters German airspace, a new message, 'FROM EDYY CTL SERVICE TERMINATED', is displayed. A communication from Rhine Control, 'ACTIVE ATC EDUU', is expected, but does not appear in the ATC Mailbox, so the crew checks and notices that no datalink communication has been established. As a result, the pilots revert to voice communication with the ATC centre at Rhine.

F/O: 'Afternoon Rhine, Skybird 380 maintaining flight level three seven zero.'

Rhine Control: 'Skybird 380, you are identified.'

A message from Maastricht ATC, indicating that CPDLC has been terminated. With no datalink message from the next control centre, Rhine, the pilots revert to VHF voice communications.

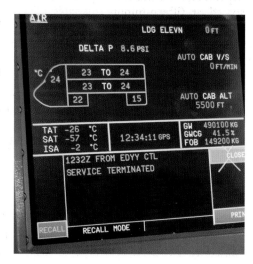

COCKPIT SECURITY

After the pilots finish their meals, the captain gets a call from a cabin crew member with a request for a young passenger to visit the cockpit. Unfortunately, by law, such flight deck visits are no longer permitted while the aircraft is in flight. The terrorist attacks of 11 September 2001, on New York and Washington, changed the world and especially the aviation industry, where security procedures and practices were tightened. Aircrew policy prior to 9/11 was one of appeasement and co-operation when dealing with hijackers. Crews were encouraged to accede to demands and discouraged from resistance or heroics. It was hoped that such a policy would result in a positive outcome for the safety of passengers and crew, which had been the case in most previous hijackings. However, the suicide attacks of 9/11 changed all that. Now pilots must not surrender to hijackers' demands under any circumstances, and the cockpit door must never be breached.

In a hijack situation, an immediate landing at the nearest suitable airport is required. Today governments are reluctant to permit hijacked aircraft to over-fly populated areas, or to permit landings at major commercial airports; instead hijacked aircraft are directed to remote airports or, more often, to military bases.

Hijackings are best prevented on the ground, and to this end all passengers are subjected to the inconvenience of body scanners and searches. Behind these visible security measures, airline companies also enforce strict security practices. Passenger meals and amenities are screened before being taken aboard the aircraft, mechanics' tool boxes are searched, and all airline personnel undergo a 'pat down' body search before being allowed anywhere near the aircraft. On some flights, armed sky marshals are carried; in the USA, commercial pilots are permitted to keep firearms on the flight deck.

CREW REST FACILITIES

Having been built primarily for long-range flying, the A380 is provided with separate crew rest rooms for use during the cruise on extended flights. The two pilots' rooms, each with climate control and an in-flight entertainment system, are situated in the space between the reinforced cockpit door and the outer 'privacy' door. In the aft section of Skybird 380's main deck is an area equipped with twelve double-decker bunks for the cabin crew. Different options are available for locating the cabin crew rest compartment, with some airlines choosing the aft upper deck or the mid-belly of the aircraft.

FLIGHT PROGRESS

As Skybird 380 is handed from one ATC controller to the next, the pilots monitor the aircraft's progress against the flight log. The times of crossing waypoints are noted, the fuel on board is checked and the aircraft position indicated on the ND is compared to the Jeppesen en-route charts. As the aircraft leaves German airspace, Rhine Control instructs the crew to contact Prague Control.

F/O: 'Prague Control, good afternoon. Skybird 380, flight level three seven zero.'

Prague Control: 'Skybird 380, you are identified. Maintain three seven zero, track direct to Abitu.'

The first officer reads back the clearance and, once again, presses the 'Direct to' button on the KCCU. The position Abitu is selected and confirmed on the MFD, and the autopilot is commanded to turn towards the control boundary between Slovakia and Hungary.

COMMUNICATIONS

Over Europe and other continental regions, VHF radio is the primary means of communication, giving clear readability, although it does have a limited range of 250nm. For long-range communications during oceanic flights, HF radios are used if CPDLC is unavailable. In the A380 cockpit, there are three communications boxes called the Radio Management Panel (RMP). Each box allows control of the three VHF, two HF and two Satcom voice systems. Internal communication between the cockpit and the crew in the cabin can also be selected on this panel, but the pilots prefer to use the handset.

Radio Management Panel (RMP). 'VHF1', at the top, is highlighted in green to indicate that the radio is active in the transmit mode. Both VHF1 and VHF2 have white lights illuminated to show that they are also in the receive mode. VHF2 is tuned to 121.5MHz, the international distress frequency.

Undoubtedly the greatest advance in aviation over the past twenty years has been the availability of satellite systems for communication and navigation. Improvements in Satcom have provided crews with crystal-clear voice communication from anywhere in the world. By pressing the Satcom buttons on the RMP, a call can be made from the aircraft to any telephone number on the ground. The crew can make calls to company headquarters or even to their families. With Satcom contact, the pilots can seek assistance from the relevant airline departments to aid making sound decisions if problems arise while airborne. In-flight medical emergencies can also be handled by the cabin crew through contact with contracted medical services. Given that the likelihood of a medical emergency is increased by the greater number of passengers on the A380, this service is especially useful.

FLIGHT WARNING SYSTEM

Skybird 380 proceeds uneventfully over the Czech Republic, Slovakia, Hungary and into Romania. As the aircraft approaches the Black Sea, cruising at FL370, an alert warning unexpectedly breaks the silence in the cockpit. An Electronic Centralized Aircraft Monitoring (ECAM) message, 'A-ICE ENG 1 VLV CLOSED', appears on the Engine/Warning Display (EWD). The alert message is accompanied by a warning chime and the illumination of an amber master caution light, 'MASTER CAUT', on the glare shield. The amber light and 'MASTER CAUT' legend are used to indicate a lower level of warning than the red 'MASTER WARN' light also situated on the glare shield. Warning signals indicating malfunctioning items are propagated by the aircraft's two Flight Warning Systems (FWSs), which form part of the ECAM system. Information on aircraft systems is fed to the FWSs for display on the EWD and SD. Any malfunction triggers the aural warning plus a visible warning on the glare shield; a malfunction message, together with the appropriate corrective checklist, is displayed on the EWD.

The master warning light button is pressed to reset the system and, in accordance with Standard Operating Procedures (SOPs), the captain calls, 'ECAM action.' This instructs the first officer to read the displayed checklist and carry out the necessary actions. In this case, the ECAM message indicates that the number-one engine anti-ice system has malfunctioned and is no longer operative. A recovery or reset of the system is considered first before the next step of reading the accompanying status message displayed at the bottom of the SD screen. On the overhead panel is a group of circuit breakers that control a variety of components and can be reset when attempting to clear a malfunction. In this case, however, there is no circuit breaker to reset to clear the condition, so the crew considers recycling the engine's anti-ice control switch. The first officer attempts a recovery by recycling the switch, but to no avail. The faulty anti-ice valve is stuck closed. A check of the Status page reveals that the number-one engine's anti-ice is unavailable for all phases of flight. Having read and reviewed the status message, the crew cancel the

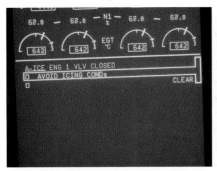

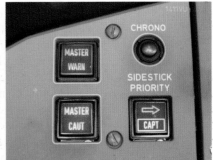

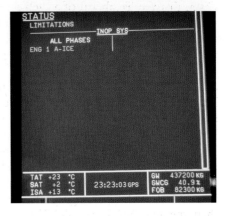

Above: An Electronic Centralized Aircraft Monitoring (ECAM) message, warning of problems with an anti-ice valve, is displayed together with the appropriate checklist actions.

Above right: Master warning lights accompany all ECAM messages.

Right: Status messages provide information on the current condition of the aircraft systems and are reviewed after any ECAM message.

Status page. As long as the problem remains, the message will continue to be displayed as a reminder whenever the page is recalled.

The crew is required to make a note that the number-one engine's anti-ice bleed-air system is inoperable and to enter the defect into the maintenance e-log book for rectification in Dubai. The entry is simply a back-up, however, since the engineering personnel would have been alerted as soon as the defect was detected, a message having been sent automatically by the aircraft's Flight Warning System (FWS) computer to the home base via the AOC datalink system. Thus the engineers have some lead time to analyse the problem and to assemble the necessary parts for rectification of the fault when the aircraft arrives.

Having completed the checklist, the pilots consult the electronic library for information on the defective component to familiarize themselves on the procedure for operating with the system malfunction. The Flight Crew Operating Manual (FCOM) is consulted on the defect, and it is noted that with the bleed valve problem, any icing condition should be avoided. A schematic diagram of the anti-ice system is also retrieved for examination. No icing conditions are forecast for the planned route and, with clear skies and a warm surface temperature of 34°C in Dubai, icing is not a concern. The next step is for any defect that may affect the landing performance to be entered into the Aircraft Status page of the On-Board Information System (OIS).

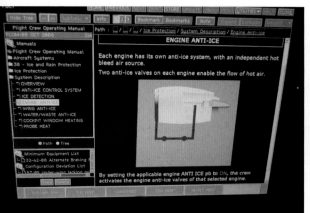

Information on the various aircraft systems can be retrieved from the library via the On-Board Information Terminal (OIT). Here the engine anti-ice system has been called up.

Limitations and memo messages are also generated automatically by the aircraft's Flight Warning System (FWS) as a reminder to the pilots.

Then the defect will be factored into the calculations for any landing performance adjustments that may be required. The crew notes that this particular defect is not listed and therefore will not affect the aircraft's landing performance.

As well as displaying the abnormal procedures and checklists, the FWS computers also generate any accompanying memos and limitations. The former, displayed in green, are produced by a switching monitor to remind the pilots that certain switches have been selected 'on', such as the seat belt and no smoking signs. Limitations displayed in blue inform the pilots that certain parameters or conditions should not be overlooked, as in the case of the anti-ice failure, where flying in icing conditions should be avoided. The FWS computer of the ECAM system is also responsible for generating the normal checklists, which the pilots select by pressing the 'CL' (Checklist) button on the ECAM Control Panel (ECP).

STEP CLIMB

After three hours of cruising at FL370, Skybird 380 enters the Turkish region over the Black Sea. So far, 46 tonnes (45.3imp/50.7US tons) of fuel have been consumed, lightening the aircraft sufficiently to allow a step climb to FL390. The first officer contacts Ankara Control by radio with the request to climb, and the clearance is given immediately. The captain selects FL390 in the altitude window on the Auto Flight System (AFS) control panel and presses the altitude knob. As indicated on the Flight Mode Annunciator (FMA), the Auto Thrust changes from 'MACH' (Speed Hold mode) to

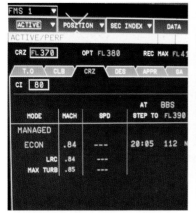

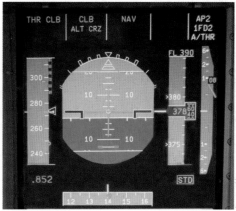

The Cruise Performance page indicates that a step climb to flight level 390 should be made as a result of the aircraft's lighter weight following fuel burn-off.

During a step climb, the Flight Mode Annunciator shows Thrust Climb ('THR CLB') power set and Flight Director pitch in the climb ('CLB') mode, with 'ALT CRZ' (altitude cruise) in the blue armed mode.

'THR CLB' (Thrust Climb mode). In the FMA pitch column, 'ALT CRZ' (Altitude Cruise) changes to 'CLB' (Climb), indicating that the Flight Director (FD) is commanding the autopilot to pitch up and hold the present Mach number in the climb. Beneath the green 'CLB' on the FMA, 'ALT CRZ' is displayed in blue, indicating that it is in the armed mode and ready to capture FL390. At FL380, the standard call of 'One to go' is made. As FL390 is approached, the FD vertical mode captures the altitude, and the FMA displays 'ALT CRZ*', the star signifying the intermediate capture. On levelling off, the display changes to 'ALT CRZ' and the Auto Thrust mode of 'THR CLB' reverts to 'MACH'.

DECOMPRESSION PROCEDURES

The flight is progressing well through Turkish airspace, the aircraft arriving at its route waypoints two minutes ahead of the flight-plan schedule. The pilots also note that the amount of fuel on board at the waypoints is greater than forecast by the flight plan and that some 300kg (660lb) of fuel have been 'made'. The savings in time and fuel are attributed to better-than-expected tail-winds and short-cuts given by ATC. As the flight proceeds across the Black Sea, the first officer retrieves the published cabin decompression procedures for the crossing of the Zagros mountain range in Iran. Crossing high ground brings with it particular challenges. If a decompression occurs at altitude, oxygen masks automatically drop for passenger use, while the captain and co-pilot don their own masks. Relying on the emergency oxygen supply alone without a back-up, however, is not acceptable and the aircraft must descend immediately to an oxygen life sustaining altitude of 10,000ft. But descending to this lower level may not be an option if the aircraft is over the Zagros Mountains, where the peaks are higher than 10,000ft. So an initial descent would be made to the lowest possible safe altitude with a step down to 10,000ft as soon as possible.

The captain reviews the decompression instructions for best use of the limited supply of emergency oxygen and briefs the first officer on the procedures to adopt in the event of an emergency descent. Skybird 380's route into Iran is on the south-easterly airway UL223. After crossing into Iran, the waypoint SNJ, a VOR radio beacon, is indicated as the critical decision point. If a decompression were to occur before SNJ, the aircraft would have to turn back and retrace its routing while initiating an emergency descent to a minimum altitude of 15,000ft until reaching waypoint (VOR) ZAJ. After ZAJ, the aircraft could make a step descent to 13,000ft. The crew and passengers would have to remain on oxygen until waypoint (VOR) RST, after which the aircraft could finally descend to 10,000ft, where oxygen masks could be removed. Then a diversion to the city of Baku, in the north, would be carried out.

If the decompression were to occur after the critical decision point of SNJ, the flight could continue in a south-easterly direction with an emergency descent initially to 16,000ft until reaching waypoint (VOR) ISN. After ISN, the aircraft could descend to 10,000ft with a diversion to the city of Esfahan. This strategy would keep the aircraft above the high ground and ensure sufficient oxygen for the crew and passengers.

While flying across the Zagros Mountains, the crew keeps a keen eye on the Minimum Off-Route Altitude (MORA), shown at the bottom left of the ND. Displayed in magenta, the MORA gives the minimum altitude required for safe flight above the highest peak within a 40nm radius of the aircraft's position. The captain's ND is selected to 'TERR' (Terrain) to display a relief map of the area. The standard procedure in the event of a decompression is to carry out an emergency descent to the lowest safe altitude, as indicated by the MORA, or to a minimum of 10,000ft. An immediate descent is essential, for without emergency oxygen, the time of useful consciousness due to hypoxia may be as little as twelve seconds at 39,000ft.

In an explosive decompression caused, for example, by the aircraft's skin being punctured by such as a tyre blowing in the wheel well, the cabin altitude would instantly climb to the cruise altitude. A misty fog would engulf the cabin as the moisture it contains condensed. Masks would automatically drop from the ceiling to supply oxygen to the passengers. After the pilots had donned their full-face oxygen masks, they would descend the aircraft to a lower altitude as rapidly as possible. The crew's oxygen mask units automatically regulate the mix of the thin ambient air and bottled oxygen, the oxygen concentration being varied according to the altitude. At 40,000ft, only pure oxygen is supplied under pressure to the pilots' masks.

As the aircraft would be cruising on autopilot, to initiate the descent the

Minimum Off-Route Altitude (MORA) is shown on the left side of the Navigation Display (ND), indicating that within 40nm of the aircraft's position the lowest safe altitude is 8,000ft.

captain would wind down the altitude on the AFS control panel and then pull the altitude knob to initiate the descent. Immediately, the Auto Thrust would retard to idle and the nose would pitch down. To steer clear of the airway, the pilot would pull the heading knob to turn the aircraft 30 degrees to the right to avoid conflicting with aircraft that could be cruising below on the same airway. (With GPS navigation being so accurate, aircraft fly directly one above the other as they track along the airway centreline.) The speed knob on the AFS control panel would be pulled to capture and maintain the speed at which the decompression occurred, as an increase in airspeed could cause further damage to the aircraft. Then the speed brakes would be fully deployed and the aircraft would descend at a rapid rate of 9,000ft a minute. The first officer would carry out the emergency descent actions with reference to the appropriate checklist called up on the EWD. When the aircraft reached the lower oxygen acceptable altitude of 10,000ft, the crew and passengers could remove their masks and breathe the ambient air.

CHAPTER 7
THE DESCENT

After Skybird 380 passes the Iranian mountains, the pilots' attention shifts to preparing for the arrival in Dubai. The Automatic Terminal Information Service (ATIS) weather and landing conditions are requested for Dubai and Sharjah airports via datalink. The 'ATIS COM' (ATIS communication) button on the Keyboard and Cursor Control Unit (KCCU) is pressed, and the International Civil Aviation Organization (ICAO) four-letter codes for Dubai (OMDB) and Sharjah (OMSJ) are entered on the ATIS request page of the Multi-Function Display (MFD). The ATIS reports are received and printed for review. Clear skies, light winds and warm conditions of 34°C await the flight's arrival. Dubai ATIS also indicates that an Instrument Landing System (ILS) is unserviceable and that the runway has been downgraded from an ILS approach to a VHF Omni-Range (VOR) radio beacon approach. The weather reported for Dubai is a typical clear night, so the pilots are not unduly concerned about the less-accurate VOR non-precision approach, as they expect to see the landing runway easily in the clear visibility.

WEATHER PROBLEMS

For most of the year, the weather in Dubai is calm with clear skies. Occasionally in the summer, however, strong gusty winds bring dust storms. Of concern during these conditions is wind shear, which is the result of rapid changes of wind speed and direction. If wind shear is reported on the approach to a runway, the best option for the pilots may be to delay the landing or to divert to an alternate airport. If inadvertently caught in wind shear during an approach, an immediate go-around is carried out. Wind shear is also associated with stormy weather, especially heavy rain and thunderstorms. In these conditions, the problem can be compounded by a 'wash out', where visibility is reduced to zero by a combination of heavy rain and the average 140kt forward speed of the aircraft on final approach.

Strong cross-winds also present a challenge for the landing pilot, as the wind can catch the side of the wide fuselage and carry the aircraft outside the confines of the narrow runway. If the landing flare is extended unnecessarily, it only takes two seconds for the main wheels to drift to the side of the runway. On cross-wind landings, therefore, the pilot must take care not to 'float' the aircraft during the landing, but should intentionally touch down firmly so that the wheels make positive contact with the runway. The allowable maximum landing cross-wind for the A380 is 40kt.

APPROACH BEACONS

The VOR radio beacon approach to land at Dubai is less accurate than the ILS approach. The ILS transmits both lateral and glide slope (descent profile) beams that provide accurate guidance on the approach to land down to a low minimum decision height of, typically, 200ft above the airport elevation. On the approach, the pilot must be able to see the runway by the published decision height for a visual landing. If not, a go-around must be initiated, in which case, the landing is discontinued and the aircraft follows the airport circuit pattern for another approach attempt, or the crew may decide to divert to the alternate airport.

In contrast to the ILS, the VOR radio beacon transmits a beam that gives only lateral guidance on the approach to land, and the pilot is required to descend on a profile by matching heights with certain distances transmitted by its Distance Measuring Equipment (DME), until a 'see to land' position is reached. The non-precision nature of this approach requires a higher minimum decision height than that of the ILS approach, in this case 890ft above the Dubai airport elevation, at which point the runway must be visible.

The Standard Terminal Arrival Routing (STAR) that feeds the aircraft from the airway's exit point of Desdi to the start of the approach at Budok, the Initial Approach Fix (IAF) for runway 30R (right), is the DESD3T

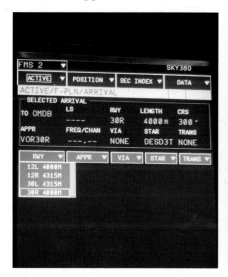

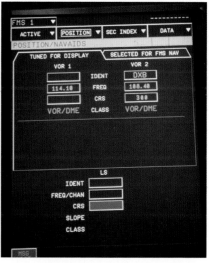

In preparation for the arrival, the STAR Desdi 3 for runway 30R is selected from the list of arrival and approach routes into Dubai.

Since a VOR-based approach is to be flown, the right-hand VOR receiver is tuned manually to the Dubai VOR beacon (DXB) as a back-up.

arrival, which is selected and activated on the MFD. Then the VOR approach for landing on runway 30R is selected and the radio beacons checked. Although the VOR beacons are automatically tuned according to the approach, as a back-up the captain manually tunes the right side receiver to the Dubai VOR (identification DXB) with its final inbound course of 300 degrees for landing on 30R. This locks the Dubai VOR in the manual-tune mode for display on the first officer's Navigation Display (ND) when selected. The approaches are usually flown by the autopilot, leaving the pilots free to monitor the flight closely.

APPROACH AND LANDING PERFORMANCE

Next the Fuel and Load page is selected on the MFD to check the fuel remaining at destination and determine the time available for holding over Dubai before the minimum fuel required for diversion to Sharjah (OMSJ) is reached. Having saved a little fuel along the way, a total of forty minutes holding is calculated as being available. On the Approach Performance page, the ambient surface conditions at Dubai, such as wind, temperature and altimeter pressure setting, are entered. On the secondary flight plan page on the MFD, the alternate routing from Dubai to Sharjah is pre-planned into Secondary Plan One in case it is required for diversion.

Using the aircraft's projected landing weight of 367.1 tonnes (364.3imp/408.0US tons), the Flight Management System (FMS) calculates the landing reference speed (Vref) – the minimum speed for landing – as 133kt. The FMS adds one third of the expected head-wind to the Vref to obtain the final approach speed (Vapp), subject to a minimum of 5 and a maximum of 15kt. Since the expected wind, blowing from 300 degrees at 8kt, is inconsequential, the 5kt minimum is added, giving a final approach speed

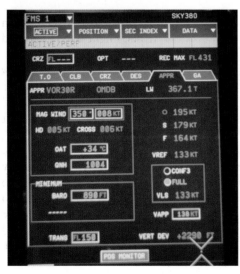

The weather conditions on the ground are entered on the Approach Performance page of the Multi-Function Display (MFD). The landing speed ('VLS') is calculated to match the desired flap setting.

The pilots use the On-Board Information Terminal (OIT) to calculate the Landing Application (LDA) performance to ensure that the runway conditions are sufficient to accommodate the landing.

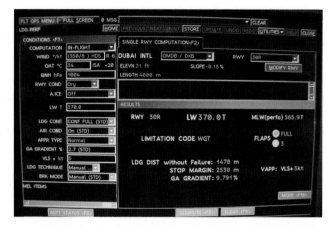

of 138kt. It may come as a surprise to many that such a heavy aircraft can fly an approach at such a slow speed. The Auto Thrust maintains the FMS programmed speeds, depending on the flap positions. A 'green dot' speed of 184kt (the most efficient flying speed at the aircraft's present weight) and an 'S' speed of 168kt (the minimum clean speed with flaps up) are displayed on the Approach Performance page.

Next the pilots turn their attention to the On-Board Information Terminal (OIT) to calculate the maximum allowable landing weight, and enter the weather and landing conditions on the Performance Landing Application (LDA) page. The maximum allowable landing weight of 565.9 tonnes (557.0imp/623.8US tons) shows the actual landing weight of 367.1 tonnes (364.3imp/408.0US tons) to be well within limits for the prevailing conditions.

CAPTAIN'S BRIEFING

The captain begins the approach and landing briefing, the Jeppesen approach and landing charts being called up from the Electronic Flight Bag (EFB) and displayed on the OIT for reference while the pilots review the procedures. Radio beacons are checked and the selections confirmed. The usual means of identifying radio beacons by deciphering their Morse code transmissions is not necessary on the A380, as the computer decodes the identification signal and displays the alphabetic codes (in this case, DXB) on the ND. The aircraft Status page is retrieved to review the outstanding defective equipment issues, and while the engine anti-ice message remains, it does not affect the arrival. NOTAMS (Notices to Airmen) for the airport are discussed and a taxiway closure noted. The charts are compared to the route details programmed into the FMS, and the plan for holding and diversion in respect of fuel is also discussed. The taxi route to the gate after landing is considered, as is the published taxiway closure, but this does not affect the route to the expected parking bay of F12. Finally, the captain sets the automatic brake to level 'LO' (low) to pre-set a deceleration of 4kt/sec on touch-down.

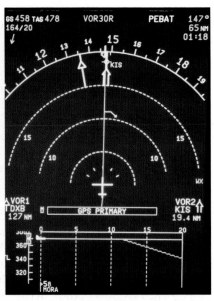

Above: On the Navigation Display (ND), the downward pointing white arrow along the track line is the point of descent calculated by the Flight Management System (FMS).

Above left: Descent checklist is completed prior to the descent.

Left: When pressed, the altitude knob sends a command to the autopilot to initiate the descent.

With the briefing completed, the captain makes a public address to the passengers, giving the updated arrival time and the weather at Dubai. After thanking the passengers for their custom, he tells the cabin crew to prepare for the arrival. Then he calls for the Descend checks. The first officer retrieves the Descent checklist on the Engine/Warning Display (EWD), reads it aloud and 'ticks off' the completed items.

THE DESCENT

At approximately 130nm from Dubai, the first officer contacts Tehran Control for descent clearance, and *Skybird 380* is instructed to descend to FL310. At the 'top of descent' mark, indicated on the track on the ND by a white arrow pointing down, the captain winds down the altitude knob on the Auto Flight System (AFS) panel to enter 31,000ft and presses the knob. Engine thrust automatically reduces to idle, as indicated by 'THR IDLE' (idle thrust) on the Flight Mode Annunciator (FMA), and the engine power gauges on the EWD wind down. The thrust levers remain in the 'CL' detent. In the second column of the FMA, the Flight Director (FD) mode changes from 'ALT CRZ' to 'DES' (descent) as the nose pitches down. The 'NAV' (navigation) mode in the third column remains unchanged.

The FMS programs a descent profile based on the forecast winds. It will follow the profile at a rate of about 2,500ft/min and plans an ideal descent speed of Mach 0.84 initially, with a transition to 311kt when lower. During the descent, the programmed forecast winds are unlikely to correspond with the actual winds experienced, so a deviation from the profile will result. To maintain the planned descent profile, therefore, the aircraft will pitch up or down to vary the speed as necessary. If Air Traffic Control (ATC) does not intervene with an instruction to level off at an intermediate altitude, the autopilot will fly the aircraft on the planned profile until it reaches 10,000ft, where it will slow to the 250kt maximum speed required by ATC in the terminal area. The descent continues until the beginning of the Standard Terminal Arrival Route (STAR) at Desdi, where the autopilot will fly the aircraft in accordance with the pre-programmed DESD3T profile in the FMS. This includes observing all the height and speed constraints demanded by the STAR.

As the flight approaches FL310, the first officer requests further descent clearance. The aircraft is still within Iranian airspace, but nearing the United Arab Emirates (UAE) Flight Information Region (FIR) entry point of Orsar. The Tehran controller instructs Skybird 380 to contact UAE for further descent clearance, even though the aircraft is still over Iran, saying that Tehran Control has no objection to the flight's further descent on the Iranian side of the border. UAE control is contacted:

F/O: 'UAE Control, good evening. Skybird 380 approaching flight level three one zero, squawking two two one one, requesting lower. There is no objection from Tehran Control.'

UAE Control: 'Evening Skybird 380, identified, clear descend to flight level one five zero.'

F/O: 'Descend flight level one five zero, Skybird 380.'

As the aircraft enters UAE airspace, a direct track is given.

UAE Control: 'Skybird 380, direct Desdi for the Desdi three tango arrival, runway three zero right.'

F/O: 'Direct Desdi, Desdi three tango arrival, Skybird 380.'

Having read back the clearance, the first officer presses the 'DIR' (direct) button on the KCCU keypad, and all waypoints ahead are displayed on the

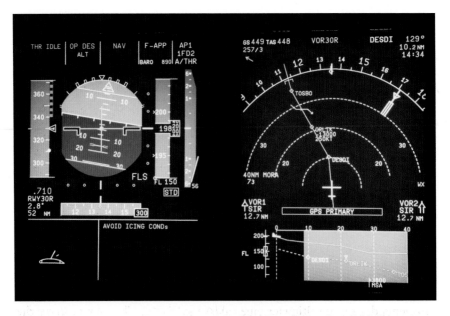

The clearance to route direct to waypoint Desdi puts the aircraft high on the descent profile, as shown on the Vertical Display (VD) at the bottom of the ND. The dotted line gives the required descent profile, while the solid line indicates the actual profile. To lose height, the speed brakes are deployed, as depicted at the bottom left of the Primary Flight Display (PFD).

MFD. Desdi is selected, the flight plan change is confirmed and the aircraft turns towards Desdi. The direct track to Desdi bypasses the intermediate waypoints, shortening the distance to run, which places the aircraft high on the descent profile. To lose height and regain the profile, the captain has to increase the rate of descent by either increasing the airspeed or deploying the speed brakes to spoil the lift and increase the sink rate. The captain decides to use the speed brakes. As they are deployed, a slight rumble caused by airflow buffeting over the wings is felt and the sink rate sharply increases to more than 5,000ft/min. As the aircraft approaches the cleared level of FL150, UAE Radar re-clears the flight for further descent.

UAE Control: 'Skybird 380 re-cleared to seven thousand feet, QNH [local area pressure altimeter setting] one zero zero four.'

F/O: 'Re-cleared seven thousand feet, one zero zero four, Skybird 380.'

The captain winds the altitude knob down to 7,000ft. On passing FL150, the UAE transition level, the pilots select the local area altimeter pressure setting of 1004hP (hectoPascals) on the Electronic Flight Instrument System (EFIS) panel and the standby altimeter using the barometric setting knobs. The captain's ND is selected to display weather, while terrain is chosen on the first officer's ND, which, on this dark and moonless night, will show high ground in the vicinity. Then UAE Radar instructs Skybird 380 to contact Dubai Arrival on 124.9MHz (megaherz).

F/O: 'Dubai Arrival, Skybird 380 Super, passing fourteen thousand for seven thousand feet, information golf.'

Once again, 'Super' is added to Skybird 380's call sign to indicate to the terminal area controller that the flight is an Airbus 380 and that a minimum separation of 10km (6 miles) is required between the aircraft and those following in the landing sequence.

Dubai Arrival: 'Evening Skybird 380 Super, descend seven thousand.'

F/O: 'Descend seven thousand, Skybird 380.'

As the aircraft passes 12,000ft, the captain observes that it is back on the correct descent profile, as displayed on the Primary Flight Display (PFD) by a magenta dot on the altimeter tape called the 'Yo-Yo'. The captain stows the speed brake levers, and the speed brake panels retract, returning the aircraft to a smoother ride without the buffeting.

Ahead, on the right, the city lights can be seen through the few scattered

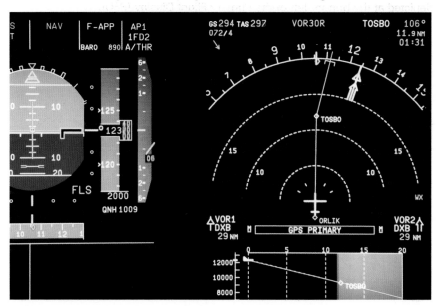

The 'Yo-Yo' profile indicator (a magenta dot in the centre of the altimeter tape – on the right side of the PFD) indicates that the aircraft is back on the correct descent profile. On the VD, the dotted and solid lines coincide, meaning that the profile is correct.

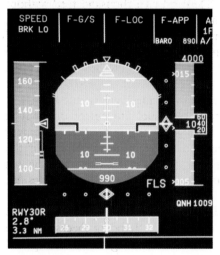

Above: The Landing System ('LS') button (below the altimeter knob) is pressed in preparation for the FMS Landing System (FLS) simulated ILS approach. On final approach, the FLS will display the inbound path to fly on the PFD.

Above left: Approach checklist is called for as the aircraft descends through 10,000ft.

Left: On the final approach, double-diamond indicators represent the FLS deviation bars instead of the single diamonds of a normal ILS approach.

clouds below. Approaching 10,000ft, the aircraft pitches up slightly to reduce its descent speed of 311kt to the required 250kt. As the aircraft passes 10,000ft, the seat belt sign, and the logo and landing lights are turned on. The approach checks are completed, and the Landing System (LS) display is selected by pushing the 'LS' button on the EFIS panel. The approach will be conducted in the FMS Landing System (FLS) mode, meaning that the FMS will generate a simulated Instrument Landing System (ILS) for display on the PFD. The autopilot flies this pseudo ILS down to the runway just like a genuine ILS. To distinguish between a conventional ILS display and the pseudo ILS display, the conventional vertical and horizontal diamonds depicting deviations from the flight path are replaced by double red diamonds. In addition, on the FMA, the indications for the pseudo localizer and glide slope are 'F-LOC' and 'F-G/S' respectively instead of 'LOC' and 'G/S'. The message 'GPS PRIMARY' is displayed on the ND, indicating that the aircraft is navigating using the accurate Global Positioning System (GPS), a prerequisite for FLS approaches. As a precaution, the first officer's ND is selected to display VOR mode, allowing the tracking of the FLS to be cross-checked against the tracking of the aircraft on the inbound course to the Dubai VOR radio beacon, which was tuned earlier.

Dubai Arrival now hands over the aircraft to Dubai Director, whose responsibility is to feed the aircraft to final approach.

F/O: 'Evening Dubai Director, Skybird 380 Super approaching seven thousand feet.'

Dubai Director: 'Evening Skybird 380 Super, descend two thousand feet. Cleared for the VOR three zero right approach.'

The first officer repeats the clearance 'Descend two thousand feet' without using the word 'to', as it can be misinterpreted as 'two'. For example, 'Descend to five hundred feet' sounds the same as 'Descend two five hundred feet'. The captain winds down the altitude knob on the AFS control panel to display 2,000ft in the window, and the autopilot follows the descent profile to that height for the final approach.

Although the clear conditions are ideal for requesting a visual approach, whereby the pilot would fly the aircraft by visual judgement on to final approach for landing, the captain decides to continue on the instrument procedure. Most approaches are either radar vectors to an ILS or, if the weather is clear, a visual approach. It is rare, however, to observe the aircraft fly a non-precision VOR approach using the FLS, so the captain decides not to miss the opportunity.

The lights of Dubai are burning brightly under the right wing as the aircraft descends through 5,000ft. The captain calls, 'Landing checks,' and the first officer responds by reading the checklist and 'ticking off' the completed

Landing checklist displayed on the Engine/Warning Display (EWD). Initially, this is completed only as far as 'LDG GEAR' (Landing Gear).

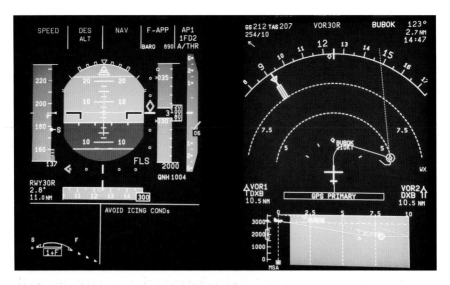

The aircraft is downwind and the speed is reducing to the Short-Term Managed Speed target represented by a red dot on the airspeed indicator (labelled 'S'). The flaps are extending to 1+F.

items until reaching 'LDG GEAR', as no further items can be completed at this stage.

'Activate approach' is the next command from the captain. The first officer selects and clicks on the 'Activate Approach' prompt on the Approach page of the MFD, which indicates to the FMS that landing is imminent and the aircraft should slow to the minimum speed for the flap configuration. The minimum speed for the selected flap, indicated by a solid red dot on the speed tape, is called the 'Short-Term Managed Speed' and is maintained by the Auto Thrust in the speed manage mode. On the captain's command of 'Flaps One', the co-pilot selects the flap lever to 'Config 1 Flaps'. This runs the slats and the flaps to position, indicated by '1+F' on the flap indicator at the bottom of the PFD. The speed reduces further to the new Short-Term Managed Speed target of 179kt.

Dubai Director: 'Skybird 380 Super, cleared for runway 30 right, VOR/DME approach, call Geveg inbound.'

Chapter 8
Approach
and Landing

As the aircraft crosses the Initial Approach Fix (IAF) at Budok, it turns on to a right base leg with a continuous descent to 2,000ft. Descending through 2,500ft, a synthesized voice announces, 'Two thousand, five hundred,' indicating that the radio altimeters have become active and that they show absolute height above the ground. Radio altimeter height read-outs are based on radio signals being bounced off the ground, the echoes giving very accurate height indications. In contrast, the pressure altimeter suffers from temperature errors, which are evident, for example, when operating into an airport like Copenhagen in wintry temperatures of -20°C. Flying over the Baltic Sea with the pressure altimeters reading 2,000ft, the radio altimeters would read an actual height of 1,800ft, indicating a pressure altimeter error of 200ft. As all altitudes and levels are flown using pressure altimeters, radio altimeters are only useful at lower heights just before landing. The synthesized voice height calls also assist the pilots in judging the landing flare. On an Auto Land approach, these heights are used by the autopilot computer to flare the aircraft for a smooth landing.

ESTABLISHING THE APPROACH

As the aircraft approaches the inbound course to the runway, the captain presses the 'APPR' (Approach Arm) button on the Auto Flight System (AFS) panel to arm the Flight Director (FD) to capture the FMS Landing System (FLS) localizer and glide slope, just as it would with a normal Instrument Landing System (ILS). The first officer selects VOR mode on his Navigation Display (ND) to monitor the capture of the inbound course to the Dubai VOR. The letters 'DXB', identifying the Dubai VOR, are displayed at the bottom left corner of each pilot's ND alongside the Distance Measuring Equipment (DME) read-out, in miles, to the beacon.

The aircraft approaches the centreline and captures the pseudo localizer, turning right to the final course inbound. The Flight Mode Annunciator (FMA) indicates 'F-LOC*' (FMS, localizer, star), which is called out by the pilots as 'F-Loc star', the star indicating that the localizer has been captured. At that moment, the altitude of 2,000ft is captured as the aircraft levels out.

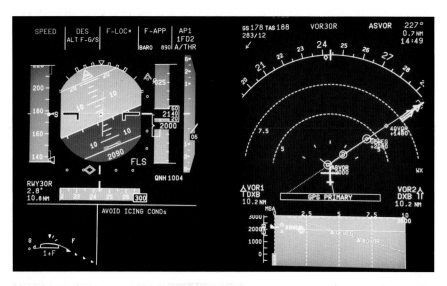

With the approach mode armed, the pseudo localizer is captured to align with the runway, as indicated by 'F-LOC*' in the third column of the Flight Mode Annunciator (FMA). 'F-APP' in the fourth column of the FMA shows the selected approach type.

The FMA displays 'ALT', prompting the pilots to call out the change. Ahead of the aircraft, the flashing green and white light of a civil aerodrome is clearly visible in the distance.

Proceeding inbound towards the final fix of Geveg, when the DME read-out indicates 9 miles (14km) – 3 miles (5km) before the beginning of the descent – the captain calls, 'Flaps Two.' With 'Config 2 Flaps' selected, the speed target drops to the 'F' speed of 164kt. At this point, the captain calls for the landing gear to be extended and for 'Flaps Three' (flaps to Configuration 3). The first officer selects the gear lever down and the flaps lever to '3'. The nose and wing gears extend first, followed by the body gear. This prevents the body and wing gears from colliding, which would occur if they were extended together. The extension sequence takes a good twenty-five seconds. The landing gear is indicated as being down and locked by five green lights on the forward panel, and by a green 'down' triangle below the flap indicator on the Primary Flight Display (PFD). Next the speed brakes are armed by pulling the speed brake lever upwards; a white band around the lever indicates that the system is armed. On landing, the eight spoilers/speed brakes on each wing deploy to dump the lift from the wings and create aerodynamic drag that will slow the aircraft, increasing the braking effect.

F/O: 'Skybird 380 established Geveg inbound.'

Dubai Director: 'Call Tower, one one eight seven five, good-day.'

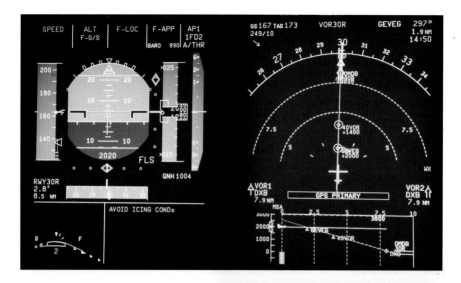

Above: 'Config 2 Flaps' is selected and is depicted by the figure '2' below the flaps indicator on the Primary Flight Display (PFD). The pseudo glide slope is armed, as indicated by 'F-G/S' in blue in the second column of the FMA.

Right: The Wheel schematic called up on the System Display (SD) shows the landing gear extending. The nose and wing gears are down and locked already, while the body gears are still in transit.

Below right: The speed brakes are armed for automatic deployment on landing by pulling the lever up from its stowed position. This is indicated by a visible white band on the lever and a blue triangle at the top of the wing indicator on the PFD.

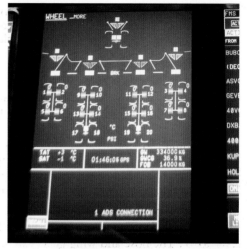

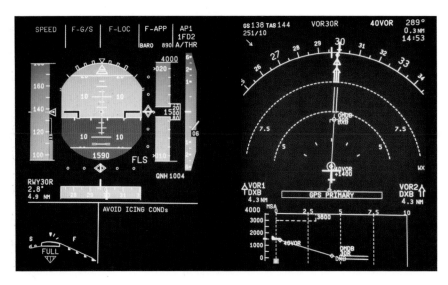

With both 'F-LOC' and 'F-G/S' captured (shown as green on the FMA), and the aircraft descending through 1,500ft, the flaps are fully extended ('FULL') and the gear is down, represented by a green triangle below the wing indicator.

F/O: 'Roger, over to Tower, one one eight seven five, Skybird 380.'

F/O: 'Dubai Tower, Skybird 380 Super, established inbound three zero right.'

Dubai Tower: 'Skybird 380 Super, cleared to land runway three zero right, wind two five zero, ten knots.'

As the aircraft captures the FLS glide slope, 'F-G/S∗' (FMS, glide slope, star) is indicated on the FMA. The captain calls, 'Full flaps,' followed by 'Complete the landing checks.' As the flaps run to the 'Config Full' position, indicated by the word 'FULL' in green on the PFD, the Auto Thrust slows the aircraft to 138kt, the speed for final approach and landing (Vapp). The go-around altitude of 4,000ft is selected in the AFS panel's altitude window in case a go-around is required. Then the first officer presses the checklist button on the ECAM Control Panel (ECP) and completes the remainder of the Landing checklist.

The aircraft is now nicely stabilized on the approach, with the autopilot flying the FLS as if it were an ILS. At this point, the captain decides to manually fly the aircraft, pressing the autopilot disconnect button on the side stick. An aural warning sounds and the red master warning light flashes, highlighting the fact that the autopilot has been disconnected. Auto Thrust remains activated for landing, as required, but the system is inherently sensitive. As the aircraft proceeds down the FLS, the Auto Thrust seems overly enthusiastic in chasing small variations in the speed, causing large

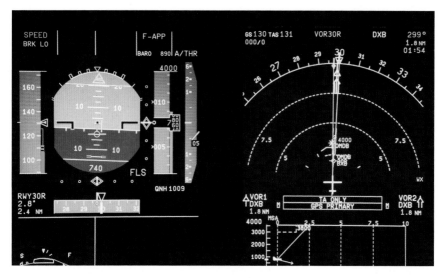

For the final visual segment of the landing, the Flight Director is turned off (blank second and third columns). The Flight Path Vector (FPV), or 'Bird', just below the centre of the artificial horizon, shows the aircraft's flight trajectory.

fluctuations in engine noise. If a sudden strong wind gust occurs during final approach, the Auto Thrust system will prevent the aircraft's ground speed from dropping below the equivalent Vapp speed of 138kt. For example, it compensates for a strong head-wind gust by increasing the power and airspeed to maintain the ground speed above the minimum – in this case, 138kt. This is called the 'Ground Speed Mini', and its function is to keep a minimum ground speed to ensure that the aircraft has sufficient momentum to escape from wind shear by going around if it occurs on final approach.

At 1,000ft, just before the decision altitude, or minimum, of 890ft, the captain asks for the FDs to be switched off and, as required on the A380 for visual approaches to land, calls, 'Track/FPA' (Track/Flight Path Angle). The first officer switches off the FDs and presses the 'TRK/FPA' button on the AFS. The FD bars disappear, and the captain flies the final approach visually, aided by the green Flight Path Vector (FPV) on the PFD. The FPV is referred to as the 'Bird' because of its shape (a green circle with horizontal 'wings' and vertical 'tail'). The FPV displays the actual trajectory of the aircraft on the PFD's artificial horizon and compensates for any wind drift.

The first officer turns the knob on the heading window of the AFS panel to the runway 'track' of 300 degrees, and this is displayed as a vertical yellow line on the PFD for pilot guidance. The track line is useful in cross-wind conditions, since the pilot only needs to 'fly' the FPV along the line to compensate for wind drift, the aircraft maintaining the runway centreline. The crabbing of the aircraft to the left, owing to the steady 7kt cross-wind, is apparent.

111

THE FLARE AND LANDING

A synthesized voice calls out the radio altimeter heights of 'One thousand', 'Five hundred' and then every 100ft below 300ft, and every 10ft below 50ft. 'Minimum' is announced as the pressure altimeter winds down past 890ft, while the captain calls, 'Landing,' to confirm his intention to the co-pilot. The aircraft continues in a steady descent at a rate of 700ft/min until 50ft above the ground, when 'FLARE' is displayed in the second column of the FMA. At the same moment, the captain eases back slightly on the side stick to reduce the sink rate for touchdown. Another synthesized voice calls, 'Retard,' to remind the pilot to move the thrust levers from the 'CL' (Climb) detent to the 'Idle' detent, thereby disconnecting the Auto Thrust system.

Any crab due to the effect of cross-wind is removed by kicking the rudder to align the nose with the runway. A secondary effect of rudder input is that the aircraft tends to roll in the same direction, because the wing on the outside of the turn moves forward in relation to the other, generating more lift as it effectively travels faster. However, a counteracting aileron input by the pilot is not required to maintain the wings level, as the flight computer does this automatically.

The aircraft settles on to the runway and the spoilers deploy. The spoiler/speed brake lever does not move, however, and the pilots must confirm deployment of the spoiler panels by monitoring the spoiler indication on the PFD. The auto brakes bite and the legend 'BRAKE LO' in the first column of the FMA changes from blue (armed) to green (activated). Besides the 'LO' brake setting, different deceleration rates of 2, 3 or full can be chosen. Also a Brake-To-Vacate (BTV) mode is available, which allows the pilot to predetermine the exit taxiway used to vacate the runway after landing. In the On-Board Airport Navigation System (OANS), the pilot selects the runway vacate point with the cursor, and the required braking deceleration is automatically provided to stop the aircraft at that exit point after touchdown.

BRAKING

There are five braking modes on the A380:

- Normal.
- Alternate.
- Emergency.
- Ultimate.
- Parking.

Normal braking employs both the 'Green' and 'Yellow' hydraulic systems, the former for the wing gear, and the latter for the body gear. The Alternate, Emergency and Ultimate back-up modes have their own independent, self-contained hydraulic systems powered by dedicated electric pumps. The

Wheel schematic on the SD, showing the landing gear brake temperatures in degrees celsius. Note that the rear pair of wheels on each body gear bogie do not have brake units.

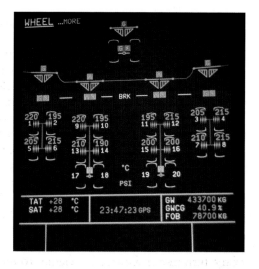

Normal and Alternate modes have automatic braking and anti-skid functions, but Emergency braking does not. If the Emergency braking hydraulic pumps fail, back-up pressure is provided by an accumulator, which stores hydraulic pressure and is good for six brake applications before its pressure depletes. Ultimate braking, the option of last resort, is activated by turning the parking brake handle to 'Park', which provides maximum brake pressure of 3,600psi (248 bar) from the pumps or the accumulators to the body gear brakes, and a reduced pressure of 1,700psi (117 bar) to the wing gear brakes. In this situation, there is a strong possibility of the body gear tyres bursting owing to tyre scrubbing – without anti-skid, the wheels will lock. Due to the normally heavy operating weight of the aircraft, brake temperatures can be

To assist braking after landing, the inner two engines are equipped with thrust reversers, shown deployed in this photograph of an Emirates A380. Note also the drooping Kruger flaps on the wing leading edge. (John Rankin)

expected to be high during most landings, and brake cooling fans are fitted, switching on automatically when brake temperatures exceed 410°C. The brake temperatures can be viewed on the Wheel schematic on the System Display (SD) by selection on the Electronic Centralized Aircraft Monitoring (ECAM) control panel.

Two thrust reversers on the inner engines (numbers two and three) are deployed to help slow the aircraft. The reversers are cancelled at 70kt, as they become ineffective at lower speeds. At taxi speed, the auto braking system is disengaged by pressing the thumb button at the side of the thrust levers. Incidentally, this button is also used to disconnect the Auto Throttle. Once again, slow taxiing is practised during turns, with not more than 10kt for sharp turns.

AFTER LANDING

The captain stows the speed brakes by pushing down on the lever, which is the signal to the first officer to start the sequence of After Landing checks. First, the taxi video and OANS are switched on, then the strobe lights and landing lights are switched off, but the navigation lights and anti-collision beacons remain on. As it is night-time, the taxi and runway 'turn off' lights are switched on. The weather radar and terrain modes are turned off, the flaps are retracted and the Auxiliary Power Unit (APU) is started to provide electrics and pneumatic supplies in anticipation of the engines being shut down.

Tower: 'Skybird 380, call Ground, one one eight three five.'

F/O: 'Roger, one one eight three five.'

The co-pilot switches frequency.

F/O: 'Evening Ground, Skybird 380 vacated runway three zero right.'

Ground: 'Evening Skybird 380, follow the greens to foxtrot twelve.'

F/O: 'On the greens, foxtrot twelve, Skybird 380.'

On the captain's command, the first officer calls up the After Landing checklist, silently 'ticks off' the completed items and, when finished, states, 'After landing checks complete.'

TAXI AND SHUT-DOWN

During night operations, taxiing is easier, as pilots are aided by green centreline taxiway lights that can be selected by the ground controller to lead the aircraft to its parking stand. The captain checks the parking bay area as

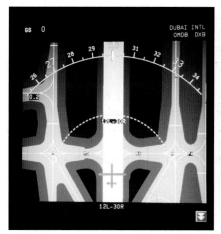

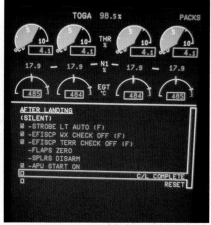

A schematic of Dubai airport on the On-Board Airport Navigation System, showing the taxiways and runway.

After Landing checklist is carried out by the Pilot Not Flying (PNF) as the aircraft taxis to its parking stand.

they approach F12 (foxtrot twelve) and confirms that the Azimuth Guidance for Nose-in Stands (AGNIS) parking guidance lights are set for the A380. The AGNIS laser sensors help the pilot to align the aircraft with the bay's centreline and to stop the aircraft at the correct point for the aerobridge connection. The taxi and 'turn off' lights are switched off before the final turn into the parking bay, as the apron area is well lit.

As the aircraft rolls to a stop, the cabin crew member in charge uses the public address system to instruct the crew members at the doors to select the doors to 'disarm'. This deactivates the emergency slide deployment system.

The captain sets the APU bleed air switch to 'on' before shutting down the four engines to ensure a continuous supply of bleed air for the air-conditioning packs. As the engines are shut down, the anti-collision beacons and seat belt signs are switched off, and the passengers are free to leave their seats. A quick 'shut-down' scan of the overhead panel is completed, and the fuel pumps are switched off. By now, the ground engineer has a headset plugged into the communication jack on the nose gear and informs the captain that the wheel chocks are in position. On receiving this information, the captain releases the parking brake to prevent seizure of the brake pads, which could occur if the brakes are too hot.

As the saying goes, the job is not done until the paperwork is complete. In this case, it is electronic 'paperwork' – the recorded flight details on the Airline Operational Control (AOC) – that has to be completed. With the captured information checked as correct, the final figures are datalinked to home base by pushing the 'Send' button. Then the Shut-Down checklist is read and completed.

If the aircraft is to be parked for some time, the Terminating checks would

The Shut-Down checklist. If the aircraft is on a short turn-around, completion of these checks is the last of the crew's actions. If the aircraft is unlikely to fly for a while, they would also carry out Terminating checks.

be carried out, but as the aircraft is on a transit and is due out in two hours' time, the Shut-Down checks will suffice. The departing crew turns off the On-Board Information Terminal (OIT) and tidies up before vacating the cockpit and leaving the aircraft. Then the ground engineer takes over responsibility for the aircraft, carrying out the routine transit checks and undertaking any rectifications required. Soon a new crew will arrive to fly the A380 to another destination.

AIRBUS A380
SPECIFICATIONS

AIRCRAFT DIMENSIONS

Overall length	73.00m (239.50ft)
Height	24.10m (79.07ft)
Fuselage diameter	7.14m (23.43ft)
Cabin width (max)	
Main deck	6.58m (21.59ft)
Upper deck	5.92m (19.42ft)
Cabin length	49.90m (163.71ft)
Wingspan	79.80m (261.81ft)
Wing area	845.00sq.m (9,095.50sq.ft)
Wing sweep	33.50 degrees
Wheelbase	30.40m (99.74ft)
Wheel track	14.30m (46.92ft)

OPERATING DATA

Flight crew	2
Engines	Rolls-Royce Trent 900 or Engine Alliance GP7200
Engine thrust	311kN (70,000lbf)
Passenger seating (typical three-class)	525
Range (with maximum passengers)	8,200nm (15,200km)
Maximum operating Mach number (MMO)	0.89
Normal Mach cruise speed	0.82–0.85
Maximum cruise altitude	43,000ft (13,100m)
Maximum altitude, take-off/landing	10,000ft (3,048m)

OPERATING WEIGHTS

Maximum ramp weight	571,000kg (1,258,840lb)
Maximum take-off weight	570,000kg (1,256,635lb)
Maximum landing weight	390,000kg (859,803lb)
Maximum zero fuel weight	366,000kg (806,892lb)
Maximum fuel capacity	310,000 litres (66,192imp/81,890US gal)
Operating empty weight	276,800kg (610,240lb)
Payload	90,800kg (200,180lb)

LIST OF ABBREVIATIONS

A/THR	Auto Thrust	ALT CST*	Altitude Constraint Capture Mode
ABV	Above	AOC	Airline Operational Control
ABN	Abnormal		
ABN PROC	Abnormal Procedure	AP	Autopilot
AC	Alternating Current	APPR	Approach
ACARS	Aircraft Communication Addressing and Reporting System	APU	Auxiliary Power Unit
		ARPT	Airport
		A-SKID	Anti-Skid
ACCU	Accumulator	ATC	Air Traffic Control
ACM	Air Cycle Machine	ATIS	Automatic Terminal Information Service
ADF	Automatic Direction Finder		
		ATM	Air Traffic Management
ADIRS	Air Data/Inertial Reference System	ATS	Air Traffic Services
ADN	Aircraft Data Network	ATSU	Air Traffic Service Unit
ADS	Automatic Dependent Surveillance	ATT	Attitude
		AUTO	Automatic
ADV	Advisory	AUTO BRK	Automatic Brake
AFDX	Avionics Full Duplex	AVNCS	Avionics
AFM	Aircraft Flight Manual		
AFS	Automatic Flight System	BARO	Barometric
		BAT	Battery (Electrical)
AGL	Above Ground Level	BLG	Body Landing Gear
A-ICE	Anti-Ice	BLW	Below
AIR COND	Air-Conditioning	BRG	Bearing
ALT	Altitude	BRK	Brake
ALT*	Altitude Capture Mode	BWS	Body Wheel Steering
ALT CRZ	Altitude Hold of the Cruise Flight Level	C/B	Circuit Breaker
ALT CRZ*	Altitude Capture of the Cruise Flight Level	C/L	Checklist
		CAB	Cabin
		CAPT	Captain
ALT CST	Altitude Constraint Hold Mode	CDS	Control and Display System

CG	Centre of Gravity
CLB	Climb
COM	Communication
COND	Condition; Conditioned; Conditioning
CONFIG	Configuration
CP	Control Panel
CPDLC	Controller Pilot Data Link Communication
CPIOM	Core Processing Input/Output Module
CPNY	Company
CRM	Cockpit Resource Management
CRS	Course
CRZ	Cruise
CSTR	Constraint
CTN	Communication Navigation Surveillance
DC	Direct Current
DEP	Departure
DES	Descend; Descent
DIR	Direction; Direct; Director
DIRTO	Direction To
DME	Distance Measuring Equipment
DU	Display Unit
EBHA	Electrical Back-Up Hydraulic Actuator
ECAM	Electronic Centralized Aircraft Monitoring
EFB	Electronic Flight Bag
EFIS	Electronic Flight Instrument System
EFOB	Estimated Fuel on Board
EGPWS	Enhanced Ground Proximity Warning System

EHA	Electro-Hydrostatic Actuator
ELEC	Electric; Electrical; Electricity
ELEV	Elevation; Elevator
EMER	Emergency
ENG	Engine
ESS	Essential
ETACS	External and Taxiing Aid Camera System
EVAC	Evacuate; Evacuation
EWD	Engine/Warning Display
EXT	External Generator
F	Minimum Flap Retract Speed
F/CTL	Flight Control
F/O	First Officer
FADEC	Full Authority Digital Engine Control
FANS	Future Air Navigation System
FAP	Flight Attendant Panel
FBW	Fly By Wire
FCOM	Flight Crew Operating Manual
FD	Flight Director
FG	Flight Guidance
F-G/S	FLS Guide Slope
F-G/S*	FLS Guide Slope Capture Mode
FL	Flight Level
FLEX	Flexible
F-LOC	FLS Localizer
F-LOC*	FLS Localizer Capture Mode
FLS	FMS Landing System
FLX	Flexible
FMA	Flight Mode Annunciator
FMC	Flight Management Computer

FMS	Flight Management System (FMCS and AFS sensors)	ICAO	International Civil Aviation Organization
FOB	Fuel On Board	IDENT	Identification; Identifier; Identify
FPA	Flight Path Angle	IGN	Ignition
FPV	Flight Path Vector	ILS	Instrument Landing System
FTAC	Fin Taxi Aid Camera		
FTO	Flexible Take-off Thrust	INIT	Initial(ization)
FWC	Flight Warning Computer	INS	Inertia Navigation System
FWD	Forward	INT	Interphone
FWS	Flight Warning System	IRS	Inertial Reference System
		ISIS	Integrated Standby Instrument System
G/S	Glide Slope		
G/S*	Glide Slope Capture Mode	KBD	Keyboard
		KCCU	Keyboard and Cursor Control Unit
GA	Go-Around		
GBAS	Ground Based Augmentation System	L/G	Landing Gear
GDOT	Green Dot	LAAS	Local Area Augmentation System
GEN	Generator		
GES	Ground Earth Station	LAND	Landing
GLS	GNSS Landing System	LAT	Latitude; Lateral
		LDA	Performance Landing Application
GND	Ground		
GNSS	Global Navigation Satellite System	LIM	Limit; Limitation; Limiting; Limiter
GPIRS	GPS Inertial Reference System	LOC	Localizer; Localizer Track Mode
GPS	Global Positioning System	LOC*	Localizer Capture Mode
GPWS	Ground Proximity Warning System	LORAN	Long Range Navigation
GS	Ground Speed	LS	Landing System
GW	Gross Weight	LVR	Lever
GWCG	Gross Weight Centre of Gravity	LW	Landing Weight
		MAC	Mean Aerodynamic Chord
HDG	Heading		
HF	High Frequency	MAG	Magnetic
HYD	Hydraulic	MAN	Manual
		MCT	Maximum Continuous Thrust
IAS	Indicated Airspeed		

MEL	Minimum Equipment List
MFD	Multi-Function Display
MIN	Minimum
MLG	Main Landing Gear
MLW	Maximum Landing Weight
MMO	Maximum Operating Mach Number
MORA	Minimum Off Route Altitude
MTOW	Maximum Take-Off Weight
N1	Engine Fan Speed; Low Pressure Rotor Speed
N2	Engine Intermediate Pressure Rotor Speed
N3	Engine High Pressure Rotor Speed
NDB	Non-Directional Beacon
NW	Nose Wheel
NWS	Nose Wheel Steering
OANS	On-Board Airport Navigation System
OAT	Outside Air Temperature
OIS	On-Board Information System
OIT	On-Board Information Terminal
OMT	On-Board Maintenance Terminal
OP CLB	Open Climb
OP DES	Open Descent
OPT	Optimum; Optional
OXY	Oxygen
PA	Passenger Address
PBN	Performance Based Navigation

PF	Pilot Flying
PFD	Primary Flight Display
PNF	Pilot Not Flying
PPOS	Present Position
PROG	Program; Programming
PWR	Power
QNH	Sea Level Atmospheric Pressure
R	Right
RAT	Ram Air Turbine
RCL	Recall
REF	Reference
REV	Reverse
RMP	Radio Management Panel
RNAV	Area Navigation
RNP	Required Navigation Performance
ROC	Rate of Climb
ROD	Rate of Descent
RPM	Revolutions Per Minute
RST	Reset
RTE	Route
RTO	Rejected Take-Off
RVSM	Reduced Vertical Separation Minimum
RWY TRK	Runway Track Mode
S	Minimum Slat Retract Speed; South
SATCOM	Satellite Communication
SBAS	Satellite Based Augmentation Systems
SEL	Select; Selected; Selector; Selection
SID	Standard Instrument Departure
SOP	Standard Operating Procedures

SPD	Speed	TRK	Track (angle)
SPLR	Spoiler		
SQWK	Squawk	UTC	Universal Time
SRS	Speed Reference System		Co-ordinated
STAR	Standard Terminal Arrival Route	V/S	Vertical Speed
		V1	Decision Speed; Critical Engine Failure Speed
STD	Standard		
STRG	Steering		
SURV	Surveillance; Surveillance System	V2	Take-off Safety Speed
		VAPP	Approach Speed
		VD	Vertical Display
TACS	Taxiing Aid Camera System	VHF	Very High Frequency
		VOR	VHF Omni-Directional Range
TAS	True Airspeed		
TCAS	Traffic Alert and Collision Avoidance System	VR	Rotation Speed
		VREF	Landing Reference Speed
TEL	Telephone		
TEMP	Temperature	WAAS	Wide Area Augmentation System
TERR	Terrain		
TFLEX	Flex Temperature	WARN	Warning
THR	Thrust	WLG	Wing Landing Gear
THS	Trimmable Horizontal Stabilizer	WPT	Waypoint
TOGA	Take-Off/Go-Around	XPDR	Transponder
TOPA	Take-Off Performance Application		
		ZFW	Zero Fuel Weight
TOW	Take-Off Weight	ZFWCG	Zero Fuel Weight Centre of Gravity
TRAF	Traffic		

INDEX